Even a Stone
Can Be a Teacher

Also by Sheldon Kopp:

Back to One: A Practical Guide for Psychotherapists
The Broken Circle
An End to Innocence
Guru: Metaphors from a Psychotherapist
The Hanged Man: Psychotherapy and the Forces of Darkness
If You Meet the Buddha on the Road, Kill Him!
Mirror, Mask, and Shadow
The Naked Therapist (with others)
No Hidden Meanings (with Claire Flanders)
The Pickpocket and the Saint
This Side of Tragedy
What Took You So Long? (with Claire Flanders)

Boulder, August '91

EVEN A STONE CAN BE A TEACHER

Learning and Growing from the Experiences of Everyday Life

SHELDON KOPP

JEREMY P. TARCHER, INC.
Los Angeles
Distributed by St. Martin's Press
New York

Library of Congress Cataloging in Publication Data

Kopp, Sheldon B., 1929—
    Even a stone can be a teacher.

    Includes index.
    1. Conduct of life.   I. Title.
BF637.C5K66   1985   158'.1   84—26695
ISBN 0—87477—341—5

Introduction © 1985 by Sheldon Kopp.
Chapters 1, 5, and 6 from *Guru: Metaphor from a Psychotherapist,*
copyright © 1971 by Science and Behavior Books, Inc.
Chapters 2, 4, 7, 10, and 11 from *The Hanged Man: Psychotherapy and
the Forces of Darkness,* copyright © 1974 by Science and Behavior Books.
Chapter 3 from *The Naked Therapist: A Collection of Embarrassments,*
copyright © 1976 by EdITS Publishers.
Chapters 8 and 9 from *Back to One: A Practical Guide for
Psychotherapists,* copyright © 1977 by Science and Behavior Books, Inc.
Chapters 12, 13, 14, and 15 from *This Side of Tragedy: Psychotherapy as
Theater,* copyright © 1977 by Science and Behavior Books, Inc.
An Eschatological Laundry List copyright © 1975 by Science and
Behavior Books.

Jeremy P. Tarcher, Inc.
9110 Sunset Blvd.
Los Angeles, CA 90069

Design by Tanya Maiboroda

Manufactured in the United States of America
BC 10   9   8   7

Contents

Introduction

I hate having wasted more than twenty years going to school. Formal education left me little of personal value other than elementary language skills and professional credentials. Much of what was taught cluttered my mind with irrelevent information. Arbitrary injunctions inhibited my imagination in efforts to learn anything new and different.

Families raise children in conformity with the conventional wisdom of their communal culture. Years of formal schooling funnel individual diversity into the same narrow channel. The intended outcome is a well-adjusted adult who will not make trouble.

In school I always felt inadequate. I was bright enough to master assigned studies, but what I was learning made no sense to me. Unaware of alternate courses of unbounded study, it took me a long time to undertake a solitary search for the particular meaning of my personal life. The uncharted explorations of this independent voyage of self-discovery involved avoiding regular routes and scrapping scheduled stopovers. In the absence of an assigned curriculum, answers offered by my earlier education were often useless.

Once I gave up pursuing the predicted proof of explanations imposed by others, unexpectedly I happened on intuitive understandings. This encouraged my voluntary suspension of disbelief in all that till then I had been taught to ignore. The immediacy of my own imagination turned out to be the most reliable touchstone for what was worth learning. It served me better than reality agreed on in advance by other people. To my delight, I discovered that openness to the undetermined meaning of each individual moment transformed ordinary external events into extraordinary personal experiences.

In an extended adolescence, the alternate routes I explored included doing dope while hanging out in Harlem jazz joints and Greenwich Village coffee houses. I spent much of my time either alone or in the company of other misfits. Fascinated by the seedy underside of life, I lost my emotional virginity by screwing around with hipsters, hustlers, beats, and any other characters queer enough to be cited by the community as crazy or criminal.

As a young adult I began listening to songs and stories from long ago times and faraway places. Hearing strange voices awakened my ears to the sounds of everyday life. Seeing shapes and colors of statues and paintings opened my eyes wide enough to watch the drama and dance performed both in the theater and on the city streets.

Eventually I explored land- and seascapes raw enough to shake the foundations of my urban upbringing. Summers spent on North Atlantic capes and offshore islands began a lifelong romance with the sea. Wandering alone along empty beaches, I picked up shells and pebbles. Attending to each one individually allowed instruction by a single stone unique even among a million others.

Later in life, I set out on more organized alternate paths. I entered psychotherapy as a patient, participated in encounter groups, and underwent instruction in yoga meditation. For a time, I chanted mantras, visualized yantras, and tried tantras. I gave up these practices only after recognizing that life itself was to be my guru.

Once having restored a beginner's mind, I found that almost anything I encountered extended my education. Avoidance of social contacts empty of personal meaning left the unfilled space of solitude equivalent to touching moments of contact with a few close friends. The mirages of marriage opened onto oases of domestic intimacy. Raising irreverent children kept life lively. Working as a psychotherapist, supervisor, and writer also allowed continuing the lifelong work on my Self. Ironically, often I am both the best therapist/teacher and the worst patient/student I have ever had.

Eventually I was forced to face death. It came to family, to friends, and to enemies. It arrived by way of aging, illness, accident, assassination, and suicide. Death approached me directly in the form of a brain tumor and a heart attack. For the time being, I have beaten back both. I am learning to live with the residual handicaps of repeated ordeals of neurosurgery and of a body battered by disease.

Even these unwelcome assaults have added to my understanding that this life is mine to live as I please. I need only lose interest in distinguishing between reality and fantasy, rational and irrational, good and bad, or between work and play. The creatively imaginative work I now play at, I once demeaned as "doing nothing."

Unexpected opportunities for enlightenment appear everywhere. Even the anticipated empty family nest is replenished as my sons return either to celebrate accomplishments or to recover from misadventures. Each brings a strange woman whom I may meet as a newfound daughter.

Illness had left me dreading that I would die not ever knowing my grandchildren. Instead I delight in the antic instruction of a two-year-old toddler named Daren, and his baby brother, Stephen. It's like having two Zen masters in residence.

Every personal encounter offers something worth learning. Any experience can be enlightening. Even a stone can be a teacher. Still, each situation requires its own solution. It remains my responsibility to recognize, to accept, and ultimately to choose that particular aspect of instruction to which I will respond.

A tale is told* of an Indian holy man who lived in a forest with his disciples. He taught them to see God in all things. One day, while deep in the forest gathering wood for a sacrificial

---

*Sri Ramakrishna. *The Gospel of Sri Ramakrishna*, Translated into English with an Introduction by Swami Nikhilananda (abridged edition), Ramakrishna-Vivekananda Center, New York, 1958, page 132.

fire, the disciples heard a voice shouting: "Out of the way! Out of the way! A mad elephant is coming!" All but one young disciple ran for their lives. Kneeling in the path of the lumbering beast, he sang its praises.

The mahout who drove the elephant screamed at him to run away, but the disciple would not budge. Seizing the stubborn student with its trunk, the elephant tossed him aside and charged on down the forest path. Bruised and unconscious he had to be carried back to the hermitage by the other disciples.

When he began to recover, the injured young man was asked by his teacher why he had not run from the charging elephant. The battered disciple protested: "You taught us that all creatures are manifestations of God. Why should I have made way for that elephant? I am God. The elephant is God. Should God be afraid of God?"

The holy man smiled. Speaking softly, he said: "Yes, my child, it is true that you are God and that the elephant is also God. But why did you not listen when God's voice called out from the mahout telling you to run away?"

S.B.K.
Martha's Vineyard,
Massachusetts
August 1984

PART ONE

MYTH AND METAPHOR

CHAPTER ONE

Just Imagine!

"... man be my metaphor."

—DYLAN THOMAS

The old philosophical question, "How do we know?" has been answered in terms of three basic ways of knowing. First, we can know things *rationally*, by thinking about them. If they seem logically consistent within themselves and with what else we know, we accept them as true. We do not believe that they are true if they seem illogical. Second, we can know things *empirically*. In this case, we depend upon our senses, truth being a matter of perceiving correctly. We can check out these experiences via objective experiments. Third, we can know things *metaphorically*. In this mode we do not depend primarily on thinking logically or on checking our perceptions. To understand the world metaphorically means we depend on an intuitive grasp of situations in which we are open to the symbolic dimensions of experience and to the multiple meanings that may all coexist, thus giving extra shades of meaning to each other.

Of course, we use all three basic ways of knowing when we make our way through uncertainties. Yet in our time, the metaphorical method has been much neglected. "Because of twentieth-century encapsulation within the epistemology of empiricism, contemporary man finds it difficult to be open to symbolic and intuitive cognition."[1] It would be fruitful to pause here to consider just what is meant by the term *metaphor,* what purpose is served by speaking metaphorically, and what special relevance metaphors might have to the understanding of what it means to be a guru.

3

Generally, a metaphor is defined as way of speaking in which one thing is expressed in terms of another; thus, new light is thrown on the character of what is being described. The simplest examples are such statements as: "Mary is an angel," or "John has the heart of a lion." Technical distinctions can be made between the metaphor and other comparative figures of speech such as the simile and the analogy. However, for our purposes, we will "take metaphor in the broad sense, as denoting any kind of comparison as a basis for the kind of illumination we call poetic."[2]

Of course, the use of metaphors is by no means restricted to the intentional writing of poetry. Such figures of speech may be used simply for the sake of expressing something more vividly, more clearly, or more memorably. Metaphor may indeed be the most natural mode in some instances. For example: "[in] the infant's mind ... everything soft is a mother; everything that meets his reach is food. Being dropped, even into bed, is terror itself. ... Children mix dream and reality ... every symbol has to do metaphorical as well as literal duty."[3]

In primitive societies as well, metaphor may be the mode. For such people the sun may be the source of warmth and life. Therefore they understand that God is the sun and that the sun is God. (Let us not be superior about such matters without remembering that in twentieth-century America some people partake of wafer and wine as the body and blood of Christ. Lest you insist that religion is always the last bastion of the primitive, remember that as an American, you can go to jail for desecrating the American flag because the flag is a symbol of the country.)

Even sophisticated, "enlightened" scientists find metaphor a useful way of formulating and solving problems. "Biologists postulate a genetic code, implying that the organic seeds of human life share the features of some secret communication system (which can then be decoded and understood)."[4]

Support for the idea that metaphor is a fundamental aspect of human experience is not restricted to the responses found in infants and in primitives. "Metaphor is the law of growth of every semantic. It is not a development, but principle. . . . The lowest, completely unintentional products of the human brain are madly metaphorical fantasies that often make no literal sense whatever: I mean the riotous symbolism of dreams."[5]

Beginning with "pictures in the head,"[6] perhaps all thinking may be said to have some metaphoric aspects, metaphor being "the source of all generality."[7] And one experiences a note of truth in the contention that "genuinely new ideas . . . usually have to break in upon the mind through some great and bewildering metaphor."[8]

In all of this, I would like to be careful not to turn away from the use of metaphor that is genuinely, intentionally, and creatively poetic. Happy as I am that metaphor "makes life an adventure in understanding"[9] for us all, I am particularly grateful to those poets who use it to tune my ears, to bring new light to my eyes, to reawaken my soul. This chapter begins with a quote from that Welsh singer of words, Dylan Thomas, who speaks a central truth for all of his poetry when he says, ". . . man be my metaphor,"[10] for it is in terms of the fundamental human concerns that he wrote. He created music and destroyed himself. Dylan is Mankind.

His most basic themes were the great polarities: birth and death, sex and violence, growth and decay. In a wonderful funny/sad, lusty/bitter poem entitled "Lament,"[11] an outrageously ribald satyr, now grown old, tells of his life, describing it with irony, gusto, and black humor. This "old ram rod," now "a black sheep with a crumpled horn," is "dying of women . . . dying of bitches . . . dying of strangers."

At the other end of the spectrum, Thomas can offer a metaphor so tender that we can love a bit more gently for having come upon it. Such a one is his description of truant youngsters at play: "the wild boys innocent as strawberries."[12]

Long ago, Paracelsus wrote that a guru should not tell "the naked truth. He should use images, allegories, figures, wonderous [sic] speech, or other hidden roundabout ways."[13] This is still good advice. It is true that metaphor "orients the mind toward freedom and novelty . . . encourages . . . daring . . .

[and] pure joy."[14] But more than that, metaphor offers a kind of vision and truth not open to computer-bank reduction.

In order to be certain and "scientific," modern psychology has thrown away much of the wisdom of thousands of years of humanity's struggle to understand itself, to be with one another, to find meaning in our lives. It has denied the immediacy of individual experience, man's encounter with metaphor. It has reduced beyond recognition the concerns that make people human. Modern psychology has lost the vision of life and growth; instead, it is preoccupied with psychopathology and conditioned responses.

Some people would return us to ourselves and take us beyond. Who is to guide us on this journey? Who will be the new guru? We cannot go further in this search without a return to metaphor, without a recommitment to intuitive, subjective experience. It may not be measurable, but it is the measure of our humanity. We must transform our way of thinking about problems, our very way of perceiving and sensing things, if need be. The change we need is "the change from imitation to expression, and from the mirror to . . . the lamp."[15] By including our personal selves once more, we will come upon the world, and upon ourselves and each other, like explorers in a new land. Wonder will be upon us once more, and we must live with it "until the world becomes a human event."[16]

It has always been true that, in seeking guidance, the many have depended on the few. In every time, in every place, there is always a "creative minority"[17] to whom others turn for leadership, for guidance, for courage, for understanding, for beauty. Answers may change; the questions remain eternal. The few who guide stand before the many, not as the ideal bearers of final truths, but simply as the *most extraordinarily human* members of the community.

Men differ, one from another, within each society. And surely they differ more radically from one culture to another.

Yet certain aspects of the human situation remain common to us all. In the final analysis, perhaps we are more alike than we are different.

Each person begins life in need of care and must find his place in the family or in the group on which he depends for survival. Each develops skills in order to cope with the physical environment and with other people. Each makes clear his identity as a child, only to be confronted with the many flowerings and sexual awakenings of puberty. Then comes the struggle through the adolescent changes of becoming an adult.

Grown-up roles and demands for achievement must be met. The pleasures and pains of courtships and marriage, the bearing, raising, and giving up of children, and the eventual decline of sexuality and vitality, all must be met. And finally, death must be faced—the death of loved ones and of enemies, and, at the center, the ever-present inevitability of one's own death.

In unspoken recognition of the turmoil that attends these crises, each culture provides institutions, rituals, and agents to help the individual through these transitions, to ease his passage. The psychotherapist is the contemporary Western agent who helps others in the midst of struggles or those who are unhappy about failing to find satisfactory resolutions to common human crises.

A spiritual guide who helps others move from one phase of their lives to another is sometimes called a "guru." He is a special sort of a teacher, a master of the rites of initiation. The guru appears to introduce his disciples to new experiences, to higher levels of spiritual understanding, to greater truths. Perhaps, in reality, he gives them the freedom that comes with accepting their imperfect, finite human situation.

Whatever it is that the guru brings, he may offer it in many different forms: he may be a magic healer, a spiritual guide, a teacher, a sage, or a prophet. These manifestations act as agents for positive change, for growth, for personal development. Each attempts to aid those who suffer from evil, illness, ignorance, or perhaps simply from youth. Each is effective to the extent that he is relevant to the needs of the time and place in which he appears.

The guru is able to pierce the vanity of the conventional wisdom of the group. He understands that reason and laws and customs of the moment offer only the illusion of certainty. The people may believe that what they "must do" or "must not do" constitutes something real. The guru can see that these formalities are no more than games. After he has passed among you, you will find that, "he sank beneath your wisdom like a stone."[18]

His is the language of prophecy, not of a fatalistically fixed future which can be predicted, but of an understanding of what man is like, of where man has been, and of where man is going. He knows that people cannot escape themselves without destroying themselves. Only by facing their fears, at times with the help of the guru, can they become what they are and realize what they might.

It has always been clear in myths and fairy tales that to flee from a prophecy is to make it come true. So it was with Oedipus. Before he was born, his father Laius was warned that he would perish at the hands of his own son. In order to escape the oracle's prophecy, Laius avoided his wife, Jocasta. He took her only once, while drinking to forget his lust. He ordered Jocasta to destroy the child at birth. She felt she could not and so gave him to a servant who was to leave the infant Oedipus in the mountains to die. The baby was found by a shepherd of King Polybus of Corinth, and the king raised him as his own.

When Oedipus had grown, he was afraid that he was illegitimate. He went to the oracle who prophesied that Oedipus would return home, murder his father, and marry his mother. Horrified by the prophecy, and knowing Corinth as his only home, Oedipus fled. It was, of course, on his escape from the prophecy that he met and killed Laius (not knowing he was his father) and later met and married Jocasta (not knowing she was Laius' widow and his own mother).

The guru, however he appears at different times and

places, is always that member of the community who understands the "forgotten language"[19] of the myth and the dream. Myths are the folk wisdom of the world. Gurus appear in every culture and they retain their qualities of wonder centuries after they have arisen, in times and places when people no longer "believe" in them. They speak to fundamental human experiences, experiences which obtain for all people at all times.

If the myth is the outer expression of the human condition's basic struggles, joys, and ambiguities, then the dream is its inner voice. It may be that by the standards of any given set of social conventions, we are "less reasonable and less decent in our dreams but . . . we are also more intelligent, wiser, and capable of better judgment when we are asleep than when we are awake."[20]

The orthodox analyst may then help the patient, whose dreams are reported, interpret those dreams and to learn what universal symbols and what personal associations make up the dream. Bit by bit, the analyst and the patient "translate" the dream. In contrast, the guru, if he is gifted, reads the story as any bilingual person might. He does not translate—he understands. He teaches this direct understanding, specifically how to to think once more in the forgotten language of myths and dreams.

Among the best of the helpers, the healers, and the guides are those who can be described as "charismatic." To have charisma is to possess the gift of grace. The Greek origin of the word relates to the Graces of mythology, those lovely goddesses of talent who brought joy, brilliance, and beauty into the lives of men. Even today, charisma may still be defined as "a free gift or favor . . . a grace or talent."[21] Further shadings of meaning have since evolved, meanings that make clear what it is to be a gifted guru.

The term *charisma* was given a religious significance when it appeared in the early Greek versions of the New Testament. In it, when Paul speaks "concerning spiritual gifts,"[22] he is no longer referring to Greek concerns of talents in music and in the arts; he is talking of such gifts from God as prophecy, understanding of the mysteries, the working of miracles, talking in tongues, and the gift of healing. But Paul added, that which gives these gifts their meaning is not the mere wonder of them but how they are used to help other men. So he says: "And though I have the gift of prophecy, and understand all mysteries, and all knowledge, and though I have all faith, so that I could remove mountains, and have not charity, I am nothing."[23]

It is not enough then that a guru be a gifted magician. His talents must not be used merely as a celebration of his powers, no matter how remarkable. His gifts find meaning only as they are used in the service of offering an opportunity to another. Otherwise he "speaketh not unto men, but (only) unto God."[24]

CHAPTER TWO

What's Your Story?

Sometimes I feel as though I am 400 years old: heavy with wisdom, too knowledgeable and burdened with the pain of it. I miss the wonder and the hopefulness that I experienced when I was young, though now I can hardly recall how it once felt. I've seen too much that made no sense, witnessed too much pain about which I could do nothing.

What sort of world is this? Not much of one: a lunatic life filled with suffering, void of meaning. Yet it is the only world there is. One can choose life, or choose death. Having chosen life, I must live it as it is. Complaining about it is part of living. But one complains without hope of life being improved as a response to the complaints: no one who can do anything about it is listening. The only ones who hear my complaints are the other complainers who are also trapped in this hollow space, this one and only available life.

This, then, is my message to myself: I can become only who I am. And I can live only this particular life that I have been given. The sole meaning for me is to go on, to feel it all, to discover as much of it as I can, to seek not improvement or even change, but the courage to see it all—every last detail—without hope of it becoming any different.

Why bother to write about it all? What for? It won't get any better. I am reminded of the old Jewish legend of the Lamed-Vov, those thirty-six hidden Just Men whose mission it was to roam the earth caring about human suffering, knowing they could not relieve it. Traditionally it was believed that so long as the heartbreaking depth of their caring went on would God then allow the world of ordinary men to continue.

I am no Lamed-Vov, no hidden saint. My anguish is more for my own place in this world than for mankind's lot. I can identify best with that Just Man who went to Sodom, hoping to save its people from sin and punishment.[1] He cried out to them; he preached in the streets and urged them to change their ways. No one listened, and no one responded, and yet he shouted his message of warning, his promise of redemption. Then one day a child stopped him and asked why he continued to cry out when there was no hope of being heard. The Just Man answered: "When I first came I shouted my message, hoping to change these men. Now I know that I am helpless to change them. If I continue to cry out today, it is only in the hope that I can prevent them from changing me." And so it is with me as well. I practice psychotherapy not to rescue others from their craziness, but to preserve what is left of my own sanity: not to cure others, but to heal myself.

I have said that my problem is I am too old, too burdened by experience. But that is a lie. In reality, I am too young, chronically a naive child of wonder with a primitive lack of understanding; I am blind, helpless, forever newborn. I look at the world with wide, uncomprehending eyes, neither trying to classify its contents intellectually, nor trying to achieve technical mastery for some practical purpose. I feel a sympathy for all that is, without understanding my own place in the time and space in which I live. I have the savage's dread of unseen foes. And like the primitive who stands for the first time before a giant Sequoia or at the ocean's edge, I am again and again filled with awe by experiences of a world which my mind cannot encompass.

I am bewildered even by the experience of my own hand. It is outside of the phenomenal "me" (located somewhere in my head and chest) and yet it is part of me. It follows my intuitive command (most of the time), yet it seems to have a life partly its own. And should I lose it, I would still be me. *Or would I?*

I am continually amazed that other people have their own selves, not quite like mine. It is so hard to believe that they are wholly other, that they are *not* me. It is bad enough (and good enough) to realize that each tree is separate from me, and so I don't have to encounter it, understand it, or deal with it. But with the cursed/blessed existence of other people, what am I to make of all of that? Sometimes I think that if we could see the world through the eyes of another person for just one moment, and look out from inside *his* skull and have a chance to contrast *his* experience with our own, surely at that moment we would go mad.

And as though it were not more than enough to deal with another human being who is not me, there is further the lovely, lunatic, frightening, unresolvable otherness of the Woman. Her presence challenges, delights, undoes, and completes my maleness. It is more than I can bear to experience her for more than moments at a time.

Sometimes just being alive feels like raw flesh . . . vulnerable, responsive, irritable, in constant danger. Those are the times when I most need to sense my place among other people, to hear their tales and know that they are mine as well. I badly need to be sure that someone can hear me; I need to receive his answering cry.

At such times, my dreams seem more reliable than my waking experiences. I have long trusted dreams as prophetic visions. I do not mean that they foretell the future, only that they illuminate the present, when my eyes are closed, so that I may see clearly. Unhampered by reason, far from the distraction of conventional wisdom, free of the distortingly protective rituals of social interactions, I can see most vividly who and where I am in my dreams. That is why I often prefer to trust my nocturnal judgment and make decisions on the basis of the morning's recollections. It seems that Jung is correct when he says our dreams are "nothing else than a message from the all-uniting dark soul."[2] Openness to my own dreams puts me in touch with the oldest, most human aspects of who I am; it helps me find my place in the community of man.

Just as *dreams* are the inner voice of humanity's most basic struggles, joys, and ambiguities, so *myths* are its outer expression. The recurrent motifs of legend and fairy tale offer concentrated images of perennial human concerns, of perceptible patterns of universally human modes of behavior. So, like my dreams, these old tales carry me beyond the limits of my personal history and back to the transpersonal stream of mankind. They retain their powerful mystery and compelling wisdom even now that we have become too enlightened to "believe" them any longer. If we are not too sophisticated, too civilized, too scientific to be open to their messages, we may still be instructed by them. To the extent that each of us is open to our own unconscious, we will be moved by the mythic legends of long-ago people who did not know any better than to believe that the world is controlled by dark forces and hidden powers. It is in this folk wisdom of the world that we can come to understand the patterns which reveal our common humanity.

So it is with the story of Pandora, Greek mythology's tale of the first mortal woman on earth. Angry at man because Prometheus stole the Olympian fire, Zeus created Pandora as an instrument of vengeance, an evil being whom all men would desire. Pandora's very name meant "bearer of every gift." Athena gave her knowledge of the arts, while Aphrodite made her beautiful. Armed with the cunning and flattery of Hermes and elegantly adorned by the Graces, she was truly irresistible. So it was that Epimetheus (brother of Prometheus) was smitten; he welcomed her adoringly to the world of mortals.

Pandora brought with her a box which Zeus had warned her never to open, not even for a moment. At last, she could not resist her curiosity any longer. She lifted the lid for one quick look at the secrets it held. In that unguarded moment, all the miseries of man flew out: into the world swarmed Greed, Vanity, Slander, Envy, and the other deadly vices. Horrified, she slammed the lid of the box. In so doing, she retained for man what was left in the box, his most basic virtue: Hope.

Had the miseries not been unleashed, surely Hope would have remained trapped beneath them. Although the evils had been unknown to mankind before Pandora's curiosity set them free, so too was man's spirited willingness to live with his imperfections hidden. Suffering makes us neither good nor bad. It is only necessary that in our wish to avoid pain and evil, we do not turn away from the growing edge to which our curiosity leads.

How are we to understand this vortex of primitive instruction? How is it that the wisdom of the ages comes in the form of seemingly senseless nocturnal visions and in the ageless entertainments of the oral traditions of folk tales? How can it be that the intuitive grasp of those most human experiences occurs in the solitude of dreams which so often seem irrational, and in the fragments of legends and early dramas which civilized man would like to have outgrown?

Jung's concept of the archetypes offers a bridge between the recurrent themes in world literature and mythology on the one hand, and the contemporary individual's dreams and fantasies on the other. However, there are distorting factors which obscure the timeless and universal meanings of the archetypal themes. Their primordial power is circumscribed by the cultural context in which they arise, bound by historical conventions of the time, and reduced by concrete ties to a particular individual's life experiences.

In the early history of man, and remaining still in those primitive cultures, dreams and myths are seen as religious realities. They constitute an unquestioned culture-determining aspect of life. As cultures "advance," the meaning and profundity of these stories and experiences are diluted by science and reason. However, science just has *not* done the job. More recently, man has become aware of some loss. Explanations do not satisfy. Knowing that this or that is *nothing but* a myth or a dream leaves us lost, with a deep sense of alienation, lost meaning, and emptiness. And so in our century, technology, once the promise of happiness, now has become the threat to our way of life, and perhaps to its very continuance. Poets, thinkers, and social scientists are open to restoring the larger significance of myths and dreams. They experience new hope in the possibility of our recapturing the wisdom of childhood, the power of innocence, the sophistication of the primitive. As a result, the new approach to myths and dreams has been used as a means of regaining access to lost existential truths. Symbolism and an intuitive approach to meaning reopen the possibility of contact with the transpersonal substance of being human. Reducing myths and dreams to simple things that we can explain, and thus feel we can understand more completely, drains the cultures which such myths and dreams once supported and to which they once provided substance. Perhaps what we are learning is to recognize that, as the poet Archibald MacLeish wrote, "a world ends when its metaphor has died."[3]

It is instructive to understand just how these powerful metaphors have been drained of their meaning by hyperrational explanations. The unquestioned tales from which primitives drew their strength, and around which they shaped the meanings of their lives, were seen by scholars as *nothing more* than stories about gods; they were not much different from the sagas in which people are the active characters. Anthropologists whose views were distorted by the Enlightenment and by the residue of self-righteous Western Christian perspectives were quick to see primitive myth as *less than* religious. Not only did they denigrate the remnants of mythic images from early societies, but they also felt that even contemporary African groups, for instance, had little more than childish tribal mumbo-jumbo to guide them. These primitives had not even recognized that there is only one God. Their symbolic cannibalistic rites could in no way be seen as equivalent of the practices of those contemporary Americans (anthropologists included) who weekly dined on the body and the blood of a dead God.

Myths separated from legitimate contemporary involvement in spiritual life, seen as less than religious, or prereligious, resulted in their being reduced to *nothing more* than the naive primitive's attempt to explain something in nature which he was really too ignorant to understand. The mythic attempts to explain how the universe came into existence—the creation myths which exist in every society—were seen in the same light as the preschool child's questions about where things come from. In other words, they were born out of ignorance and curiosity. No longer could they be understood as rising from the appreciation of man's perennial lostness in a universe filled with powers and having origins which man can in no way tie down and of which he can never be sure.

Only recently have we become aware that science *will not* save us, that reason is a whore who misleads us, that disillusion is the keynote. People have once again begun to take seriously their myths and dreams as expressions of striving for a total world view and for an interpretation of what is meaningful in their lives and as serious attempts to integrate experience and reality. Existentialism arose in Europe when humanity's hopes and dreams had been shattered by yet a second world war, one which involved genocidal barbarism, too grotesque to be comprehended. It was then that Kierkegaard was rediscovered, that Plato and Augustine were viewed as more meaningful than Aristotle and Aquinas as guides to understanding how we live. It was then that Sartre, Heidigger, Jaspers, and the rest made their voices heard, questioning the very ground of being, shaking the philosophical world, disowning the traditional metaphysical categories, and setting the world of rational scientific enquiry on its pompous ass. It was then that the emerging mythologists of our age could make their impact felt. It was then that the emerging mythologists of our age could make their impact felt. It was then that Alan Watts, the wandering minstrel of Zen and mysticism, could define myth simply and powerfully as "an imagery in terms of which we make sense out of life."[4] It was then that Freud's reductionism, his use of myths to explain away the depth and power of human experience, could begin to give way to Jung, who now suggested that dreams were visions or *images of meaning rather than symptoms*, that they constitute a magic mirror which could unify and transform our experience.

Perhaps the most extraordinary mythologist of our age is Joseph Campbell. He has gathered the old tales—maintaining the original richness of their vision—and once again raised mythology to its original status of spiritual adventure so profound as to be a matter of life and death. In an attempt to understand what myth is about, Campbell explores four functions of mythology.[5] The first function is the *mystical* or *metaphysical*, in which man attempts a "reconciliation of consciousness with a precondition of its own existence ... the monstrous nature of this terrible game that is life." Within this function are our struggles with the experience of living a life that is fundamentally unmanageable, incomprehensible, and ultimately sorrowful. How are we to make our way on such a pilgrimage, grappling with guilt, bewilderment, and impotence, unless there are myths to redeem the human consciousness from its tragic sense of being overwhelmed and lost?

Campbell cites *cosmology* as the second function of mythology. By this he means that people need a way of rendering an image of the universe in order to make sense of where they live. The myth formulates such an image that is in keeping with the science and culture of the time; it provides a sense of unity so that whatever one comes in contact with in this life can be recognized as part of "a single great holy picture."

The third function of the myth, which Campbell calls *sociological*, is defined as a way of "validating and maintaining some specific social order." Possibilities for corruption are apparent as kings and priests can invoke the profound experience of dreams and myths in order to keep people in their place while allowing those in authority to increase their power. So it is that James Joyce has Ulysses tap his brow thoughtfully, at one point, and declare "in here it is I must kill the priest and the king."[6]

Campbell's fourth function of mythology is *psychological*. Here he sees a myth as a guide and a support to individuals from birth to death and through the difficult transitions which human life demands. This is perhaps the major function for Campbell, since he sees sociological and cosmological orders as varied and those functions of mythology as contingent on the order of the time. Yet he feels there is an irreducible biology of the species in which all humans face the same inherent psychological problems. His emphasis is on the overly long period of immaturity and dependency and on the consequent difficulties in crossing the threshold to adult responsibility—the difficulty in this "second birth," which is indeed a social birth. So Campbell tells us "the fourth function is to initiate the individual into orders of his own psyche, guiding him toward his own spiritual enrichment and realization."

The ways, then, of understanding the functions of myths are many. Perhaps in the long run each way is no more than a contemporary myth—a fairy tale that comforts us as we wander through the ultimately unresolvable jungle of a darker, more dangerous, and more overwhelming life than we prefer.

As for myself, one of the ways to conceive and understand such matters is via C.G. Jung's concept of *archetypes*.⁻ For Jung, the archetypes are biological patterns of behavior, modes of perception, and ways of experiencing life which have always shaped humanity's own sense of the world. They are unconscious ways of apprehending life, evident to us only in the effects they produce. These effects typically are universal phenomenological patterns which can be recognized in the recurring configurations of situations and sorts of figures which "shape the way human beings experience themselves, others, and the world at large."⁸

The familiar motifs which repeat themselves again and again in dreams and in myths include such primordial images as the original Creation, the Great Mother both as fruitful womb and as devouring destroyer, the Great Father as Lord of Heaven, wise old man, and as wrathful judge, and the Child as the link with the past. These are the insoluble mysteries of the relations between male and female, darkness and light, heaven and earth—the groundwork of existence that makes itself known, as does the emergence and the adventures of the Hero. The myth of the dying and resurrected hero has long been used as a series of images to express the experience of the living rhythm of natural events such as the daily rising and setting of the sun.

Powerful images such as these have always dwelled in the mysterious shadow of the collective unconscious, subtly shaping the human's sense of himself, of his world, of Nature itself.

These archetypes are not inherited ideas, so much as they are inherited modes of psychic functioning and biological patterns of experience. Each person is, of course, subject to the particular experiences which make up his own personal history. But each individual also stands in relation to all others, by whatever other time or place, dominated by transpersonal modes by which all people live. The archetypes which bridge the gap between man and man "resemble the beds of rivers; dried up because the water has deserted them, though it may return at any time. An archetype is like an old watercourse along which the water of life flowed for a long time, digging a deep channel for itself. The longer it flowed, the deeper the channel, and the more likely it is that sooner or later the water will return."[9]

It is possible, of course, to try to understand dreams as nothing more than the epiphenomenal expression of physiological processes, or at most as a curiously fragmented and poetically condensed experience of any individual's residue of the day's events, perhaps motivated by unconscious unexpressed childhood wishes. So too, we can attempt to construct a natural history of gods and heroes, in which "myth means nothing other than the report by ardent enthusiasts of that which has befallen them."[10] But to me, objectifying reductions such as these dilute the transpersonal richness of the human experience which the colorful metaphors of dream and myth so awesomely enhance.

I do not know what it is *really* all about. It has been a long time since I believed in Reality. I prefer the loveliness and the terror of my subjective experiences to those coldly scientific explanations which in the long run turn out to be no more real, and far less fun, than my own fantasies and musings. And so it is that for me the Jungian archetypes provide a richly dramatic, intensely colorful trip. What more can I ask of any life-enhancing adventure? The meaning of archetypes may not help me to understand the human condition any better than I have up to now. It is enough that they allow me to experience it more deeply, more fully, with all senses open to the quality of my movement through this, my one and only life.

PART TWO

TALES OF
WONDER

CHAPTER THREE

Something Special

People in our culture respond harshly to others who make mistakes in social situations. When an adult appears flustered, others often interpret it as a sign of weakness, of low status, of immaturity, or of hiding something unenviable. Understandably, when we blunder in the presence of others, we learn to conceal our inability to cope. Ironically, the blunderer often unwittingly reveals the discomfort of his predicament with the very means by which he tries to hide it: "the fixed smile, the nervous hollow laugh, the busy hands, the downward glance that conceals the expression of the eyes."[1]

This normal social need to conceal embarrassment is heightened in the person who has been shamed excessively as a child. Neurotic character styles of timidity and avoidance may even be developed.

The result is a partially unlived life. A person who has been injured in this way simply cannot afford to risk participation in situations where this vulnerability might be revealed to others. Characteristically, the individual assumes that this openness to the pain of ridicule is singular. It is believed that other people are not as likely to appear foolish from time to time. Others are considered tougher and more competent.

This self-conscious preoccupation with being specially sensitive increases the person's sense of isolation, peculiarity, and loneliness. How sad to feel like a misfit, without knowing that ultimately we are all misfits. Basically we are not different from one another. None of us is able to cope every time with life's unexpected demands. The neurotically shy person's timid style is excessive in proportion to his belief that there is something specially wrong with him.

I do *not* mean to suggest that there is no such thing as normal shyness. The reserved manner of the introvert is probably part of the inborn psychological orientation, the naturally greater comfort with the inner world of private experiences. Furthermore, all cultures seem to promote some modesty or diffidence as a way of protecting communal living from the needlessly abrasive assault of self-centered, raw hedonism. I suspect that this is an evolutionary development by which individuals have come to compromise some portion of their inherent egocentricity in the interest of species survival.

The neurotic shyness of those who have been overly shamed early in life is another matter. When such a person grows up, the painful yoke of bashfulness and timidity hangs overhead. Some (like myself) cover this with mock boldness. But, beneath the surface is a chronic fear of other people.

The excessively shy person is usually very self-conscious in negative, self-demeaning ways. The individual feels "unwanted, unloved, ugly, different, uninteresting, lonely or neurotic."[2] Consciously fearing rejection, this person will do almost anything to avoid risking it. As a result, the individual is usually silent, hypersensitively monitoring words and gestures. This is especially true in the presence of strangers, members of the opposite sex, or others who may judge. When this person does try self-expression, he or she is likely to be hesitant, needlessly soft-spoken, ingratiating, and apologetic. Whenever possible, the individual simply will try to avoid contact with others.

This self-protective overreaction does *not* accompany normal shyness. A person who is *not* neurotically shy understands that it is the external situation that contributes to embarrassment, rather than some individual defect. Unlike the shy neurotic, this person has come to learn that these anxieties are triggered by individual reactions to particular people and situations. The normally shy individual also understands that others are probably subject to equivalent vulnerability.

Neurotic shyness constitutes a significant portion of the needless suffering borne by the men and women who seek my help in psychotherapy. Most patients complain of fear of rejection as a central source of apprehension and pain. Such a person is astonished to discover that the true underlying problem turns out to be quite the opposite.

The shy neurotic cannot overcome excessive shyness without first understanding that he fears *not* rejection but acceptance, *not* failure but success. The individual begins to go after what he wants out of life. When such action results in acceptance and good treatment by other people, this individual becomes very uncomfortable. This person feels undeserving of such unfamiliar achievement and acceptance; he or she has unwittingly learned to discredit these pleasurable experiences. A poignant early expression of this self-defeating attitude occurs during the first phase of psychotherapy. The neurotically shy patient cannot believe that I or anyone else could accept him as he is. Encouraging the patient to hold on to the comforting protection of this distrust for as long as necessary, I promise to try not to accept the patient any more than can be tolerated.

Anything that makes the individual feel worthwhile calls forth the echo of the mother's voice, which demands a questioning of presumption. The patient can almost hear her demand, "Just who do you think you are?" Believing even for a moment that he is satisfactory as a human being evokes the underlying shameful feeling that too much has been presumed.

Often the result is a largely wasted life, foolishly misspent in worrying instead of doing, in giving up the pleasures of living so as to avoid taking on the risks of disapproval. T. S. Eliot memorably described the sadly comic restrospective of a too-proper middle-aged man who looks back over a neurotically shy life that was empty of vitality.

Eliot's anti-hero, J. Alfred Prufrock,[3] laments over lost opportunities even as he hesitates to take any further risks. At each new possibility he intones, "Do I dare?" and "Do I dare?" He must not take the chance of disturbing the universe. Each moment of decision is followed by a moment of revision. A minute later, he reverses his thrust forward, retiring once more into his customary shyness.

When all is said and little is done, he has "measured out [his] life with coffee spoons." Better many cautious omissions than a single bold commission for which others' eyes might "fix you in a formulated phrase." He wonders nervously what he might dare to eat, how he might dare to part his hair. His life is not what he meant it to be at all. Yet shy as he is, how should he presume? Just who does he dare think he is?

The unhappiness that accompanies neurotic shyness may be further complicated by the development of the self-protective veneer of false pride. For those of us who have not worked through the effects of shame as children, the embarrassments of everyday life loom catastrophically large. Defensive pride tempts us to conceal our errors, to deny that we are even capable of the same mistakes that everyone else makes.

For some of us, the avoidance of direct and immediate confrontation and the confession of our screw-ups is like buying an article on the installment plan: we avoid the pain of making full payment on the spot only to find that we are then burdened by exorbitant interest rates on payments that seem to go on and on.

Guy de Maupassant's short story "The Diamond Necklace"[4] is a classic example of the high price of false pride. It is the story of Matilda, a woman tortured and angered by a shamefully ordinary life because she does not possess the luxuries and delicacies which she insists befit her station.

One day, she is invited to a ball at the residence of the Commissioner of Public Instruction. She cannot look forward to this occasion because she has nothing grand to wear. She feels humiliated. Her husband suggests she wear natural flowers, but Matilda feels she would be disgraced by anything less than grand jewels. She weeps for days from chagrin and disappointment. She is tempted not to go at all. Finally she yields to her husband's suggestion to borrow some jewels from a wealthy friend.

Matilda's friend lends her a superb diamond necklace. Delighted to be able to present the grand image that she feels is expected of her, she attends the ball. By the end of the evening Matilda discovers that she has lost the necklace.

Ashamed and unwilling to face her friend, she and her husband withdraw their savings and deeply go into debt to borrow more money in order to replace the 40,000-franc diamond necklace. The substitute necklace is returned to the friend; Matilda never has to expose her carelessness.

For the next ten years, Matilda and her husband work day and night and do without the ordinary pleasures they could once afford. At last they pay off the debt, and the accumulated usurer's interest as well. Matilda

> seemed old now. She had become a strong, hard woman, the crude woman of the poor household. Her hair badly dressed, her skirts awry, her hands red, she spoke in a loud tone, and washed the floors in large pails of water. But sometimes, when her husband was at the office, she would seat herself before the window and think of that evening party of former times, of that ball where she was so beautiful and so flattered.[5]

Her life had changed over a small matter, but at last the debt was paid. Now after avoiding her friend for so many years, Matilda visits her once more:

> Her friend did not recognize her and was astonished to be so familiarly addressed by this common personage.
>
> "... How you have changed—"
>
> "Yes, I have had some hard days since I saw you; and some miserable ones—and all because of you—"
>
> "Because of me? How is that?"
>
> "You recall the diamond necklace that you loaned me to wear to the Commissioner's ball."

"Yes, very well."

"Well, I lost it."

"How is that, since you returned it to me?"

"I returned another to you exactly like it. And it has taken us ten years to pay for it. You can understand that it was not easy for us who have nothing. But it is finished and I am decently content."

[Her friend] stopped short. She said: "You say that you bought a diamond necklace to replace mine?"

"Yes. You did not perceive it then? They were just alike."

And she smiled with a proud and simple joy. [Her friend] was touched and took both her hands as she replied:

"Oh! My poor Matilda! Mine were false. They were not worth over five hundred francs!"[6]

My parents started me down my own painful path of shame and false pride. My parents are no longer responsible for this trip that I sometimes continue to make. Now the enemy is within. It is my own overblown ego that shames me. It is I who still sometimes arrogantly insists on higher standards for myself than I would impose on others. How much easier to accept the flaws in others than in myself. To the extent that I cling to being special in this way, I remain stuck with the tediously painful life of the perfectionistic striver. I must get everything right, all the time, or suffer shame. It is far too heavy a price to pay for maintaining the illusion that I might be able to rise above human frailty.

At such times, I trade acceptance of myself as an ordinary human being for the idealized image of the special person I might yet become. I give up being satisfied with myself as a pretty decent, usually competent sort of guy who, like everyone else, sometimes makes mistakes and plays the fool. Instead I insist that if only I tried harder, really cared, truly wanted to, I could become that wonderful person who could make my deceased parents happy. Then they would approve of me. I would be the best. *Everyone* would love me.

CHAPTER FOUR

Manners and Morals

"Who are *you?*" said the Caterpillar.

This was not an encouraging opening for a conversation. Alice replied, rather shyly, "I—I hardly know, Sir, just at present—at least I know who I *was* when I got up this morning but I think I must have been changed several times since then."

"What do you mean by that?" said the Caterpillar, sternly. "Explain yourself!"

"I can't explain *myself*, I'm afraid, Sir," said Alice, "because I'm not myself, you see."

"I don't see," said the Caterpillar.

"I'm afraid I can't put it more clearly," Alice replied very politely, "for I can't understand it myself, to begin with; and being so many different sizes in a day is very confusing."

"It isn't," said the Caterpillar.

"Well, perhaps you haven't found it so yet," said Alice; "but when you have to turn into a chrysalis—you will some day, you know—and then after that into a butterfly, I should think you'll feel it a little queer, won't you?"

"Not a bit," said the Caterpillar.

"Well, perhaps *your* feelings may be different," said Alice: "all I know is, it would feel very queer to *me.*"

"You!" said the Caterpillar contemptuously, "Who are *you?*"

Which brought them back again to the beginning of the conversation.[1]

Dissatisfaction with her lot, combined with restless curiosity, led Alice to tumble into the rabbit hole. Her fall into the seemingly mad world of Wonderland, and her conversations with its zany inhabitants provided experiences so disarming that they began to undermine her politeness, her reasonableness, indeed her very identity as a reliably socialized person.

The presence of other human beings offers a continuous

challenge to the face we would present to the world. Each of us has been taught to maintain some measure of constraint over our primitive appetites and to present at least the appearance of sociability and self-control. The virtues of good character (however they may vary from group to group) are supposed to be in evidence. Some element of respect for the other—of cooperation, of candor, and of modesty—is expected. A certain modicum of civilized demeanor is demanded as we play out the masked dance of social accommodation.

We are to act as though we are not driven by powerful biological urges, not haunted by dark primitive images—as though our social identities represent who we really are. In order to maintain this acceptable sense of theater, social interaction is replete with ceremonies, conventions, and ritual dialogues which preserve the gloss of civilization.[2] Infractions and deviations which either intentionally or inadvertently reveal our underlying primitive natures are subject to censure and are quickly corrected by remedial interchanges. So it is that the powerfully primordial mythic images which guide human behavior remain hidden behind a facade of mannered reasonableness.

How often it becomes apparent that our gloss of civilization—no matter how valuable, how well-articulated, how strongly supported by philosophical and religious superstructures—remains a thin and tentative veneer. Modern humanity, those post-Enlightenment creatures, like to think of their natures as being determined primarily by psychological and cultural forces. But recent investigative and speculative scrutiny of the human species makes it clear that much of our behavior is biologically based, like the rest of the animal kingdom. The writings of Ardrey, Lorenz, Tiger and Fox, Goffman, and Hall[3] support the image of man as an imperial animal, guided by hidden dimensions which are determined by evolutionary development and mediated by genetic codes—all of which support instinctual patterns of mating, fighting, play and politics. We would like to view our interactions as based upon higher sentiments, on ideology, on moral pirnciples. Yet very often our behavior can be better understood as a product of territoriality, of unwitting biological patterns, of aggressive animal imperatives. Often we act like the animals we are. The only significantly human expression in many instances is the way in which we explain our base instincts.

The success of William Golding's best-selling novel, *Lord of the Flies*,[4] reflected our dim awareness of and fascination with the evil hidden within each of us. This lovely but grotesque tale describes nice, gentlemanly prep-school boys who find themselves stranded on an undeveloped island. Within a matter of days, they become warring primitives, frightening us by acting out the desperate and secret needs which most of us meet only in our nightmares.

But this is only a novel, you may insist, merely one man's literary invention. Not so! During the London Blitz of World War II (the "good war"), many ordinary, "normal" British youngsters were evacuated from the city in order to protect them from the nightly bombing raids. These "Infants without Families,"[5] as Anna Freud and Dorothy Burlingham called them, were placed in residential nurseries and in decent, well-run communal foster homes, generated as Colonies of the Foster Parent's Plan for War Children, Inc. Most of the children were placed on a temporary basis. It was fully expected they would be returned to their waiting families as soon as it was safe.

These healthy pre-schoolers were well-fed, clothed and housed, given benevolent adult supervision. But unfortunately, they were made to suffer the experience of life without family. Some of these children developed inordinate patterns of lying, stealing, fighting and extortion. Other children were treated as menaces against whom methods of desperate defense had to be adopted. Absence of family support and protection revealed survival patterns in these youngsters not unlike those of any desperate animal.

The patterns revealed in these British residential nurseries are by no means found only in *children* under stress. I cite these incidents first because our sentimental notions about children's behavior make these data all the more shocking. But adults, indeed whole cultures, can suffer similar deterioration. A recent dramatic and well-researched example can be found in the work of the noted anthropologist, Colin M. Turnbull. His book, *The Mountain People*,[6] describes his personal experiences with the *Ik*, a Ugandan hunting and gathering tribe. At one time, these people formed a decent, generous, stabel society. Due to African nationalistic politics, they were moved from their supportive, familiar hunting environment to a barren, waterless, game-free mountain territory in which the government decided they should become farmers.

Less than three generations in this alien, inhospitable, punishing setting left their culture in ruins and their "humanity" almost nonexistent. "Their mountain villages were far from livable; the food was uneatable because there was not any, and the people ... (became) as unfriendly, uncharitable, inhospitable and generally mean as any people can be." Compassion, love, community feeling, and family life virtually disappeared. Children were abandoned at age three and forced to fend for themselves. Those who survived became devious and dishonest adults who sadistically laughed at the pain of their fellow tribesmen. The old (hardly any survived beyond age twenty-five) were deserted but not before the younger, hardier ones (sometimes the older ones' own children) robbed them of whatever meager possessions they still had; sometimes they even forced half-chewed food from their desperately closed mouths. Though our situation is different, Turnbull wonders about the ultimate effects on humanity of contemporary Western stress, anonymity and cold self-interest.

A recent study on "The Psychological Power and Pathology of Imprisonment"[7] is chillingly prophetic with regard to the tenuousness and fragility of our enlightened, humanistically civilized ways. Only two years ago a Stanford professor of psychology created a simulated prison in the basement of the department's laboratory and classroom building. Normal young men were paid to be experimental subjects; arbitrarily they were assigned the roles of prisoners and guards. The planned two-week experiment was terminated on the sixth day because of the terrifying results: the subjects could no longer distinguish their roles from their individual selves in the simulated setting. Many of the "guards" soon became sadistic and tyrannical in their arbitrary use of power, and even the "good guards" would not interfere with the abusive behavior of the "bad guards." The "prisoners" panicked, became depressed and ruthless and sold out one another. In both groups, spirit and ethics deteriorated quickly and irrevocably. The impact of the experiment's results was so powerful that the findings were presented to the U.S. House of Representatives Committee on the Judiciary in hopes that people would become aware of the dangerous influence of the prison setting and the need for radical reform. It was proved that the civilized veneer of human nature cannot bear the strain.

We take for granted so many comforting parameters of our "natures," our standards, our ways. They do not seem so reliable to me. I am reminded of (haunted by) an experience a few years ago when I entered a hospital to undergo major surgery. I was admitted as a competent, self-respecting adult, a husband-father-friend-psychotherapist-writer, an altogether substantial member of the community. Within days, I was a frightened, dependent child and a hapless, dilapidated wreck as well. How could I know when I signed myself in, determined to take responsibility for this segment of my life, that I could be moved to tears when told by a nurse (whom I did not know) that I had a "good bowel movement" that day?

There are, I suppose, implications in this incident for the development of neuroses when parents don't give their children enough. When children don't get what they need in order to survive, emotional priorities get re-sorted and the luxury of seeking "higher things" is no longer a possibility. Instead, the children must scramble for survival and they must transform whatever they can get into their own articles of value.

I would like to point out that much of what seems corrupt, evil, brutal and grotesque about the underlying biological patterns is really only cast in that light because of our romantic notions of how wonderful it is to be "human." Even disastrous, desperate survival situations sometimes bring out lovely biological patterns as well. For example, in a crisis such as fire, flood, or political disaster, unsuspected strength, courage, loyalty and devotion often emerge. I hesitate to emphasize these parameters at the beginning because of my cynical expectation that most readers will grab at these examples (which support their most comfortable self-images) and avoid the more painfully threatening revelations.

In a recent group therapy session one man told of being moved by a television program that depicted night predators through a naturalist's eye. (In it, a pack of hyenas separated a hornless, month-old baby rhino from its mother so it could be devoured. The baby rhino escaped.) The group was pleased and relieved at the Disney-like ending to the harrowing tale, but the teller then pointed out that the baby escaped only for that night. At sunset the following day, the hyena-pack returned for another try at the kill. There were concerned murmurs from the group members. I asked why no one but me rooted for the hyenas. It was, after all, "God's way."

Some patients tried to help me overcome my "defensive hard shell." But in truth, I was only playing (in my savage way). Ordinarily, I feel no more committed to the predator than to the prey, except when I am temporarily living out one or another aspect of my own life. The world seems to me neither good nor bad; it is the way it is—a random entropic non-pattern to which we each bring meaning. I am certainly willing to take on a strong sense of theater from time to time and pretend that there are heroes and villains. But, only to intensify the experience of my journey across this stage—a stage that has many exciting possibilities, yet lacks audience, script, and direction. Like Alice, I make my way as best and as foolishly as I can through this bewildering life.

Similar to other wonderlands, psychotherapy is an effective interruption of old behaviors partly because of the therapist's willingness to operate without engaging in such remedial work.

This personal transparency combines with his limited participation in the protective social ritual. Unchecked by such constraints, the therapist and patient are plunged into primitive personal intimacy, surging with the emotional power of their surfacing transpersonal mythic patterns.

Within the frame of reference of everyday social interactions, therapy has the kaleidoscopically lunatic perspective of Alice's Wonderland. The topsy-turvy quality of the relationship has been described satirically as one in which the therapist is always one-up on the patient. The reciprocity of their superior and inferior positions is maintained crudely by the patient's defensive demands and subtly by the therapist's technical maneuvers. The disarming interplay has been described as one in which "the patient insists that the analyst be one-up while desperately trying to put him one-down, and the analyst insists that the patient remain one-down in order to help him to learn to become one-up."

The patient first submits to this uneasy balance by voluntarily seeking my help, by seeing me at my convenience and by paying me a great deal of money. The patient must say whatever comes to mind without regard to rationality, appropriateness, or social decency. I need say nothing, and often I don't. What's more, it is agreed at the outset that the patient often will not know what he is *really* trying to say, since he is guided by often unaware motives, while it is assumed that I am an expert about such matters. My reactions to my patient's behavior are "interpretations" while the patient's evaluations of me are considered "fantasies."

On the other hand, when the patient accepts that I am a technical consultant, I may insist that he consider my feelings as those of just another struggling human being. I am the detached expert who is just doing his job and who does not care whether or not the patient "gets better." At the same time I am there as a caring person who offers help but who doesn't know any more than the patient about how people ought to live.

The apparent perversity of my shifting attitudes has a hidden meaning; it would lose its value if directly revealed to the patient. The therapeutic judo of these tactics is aimed at the interruption of the patient's self-restricting, risk-avoiding character defenses, and of the face-saving gloss of the individual's mannered social interactions. My shift to being another vulnerable human—one who is there to tell his own tale—is my willingness to be a companion to the patient in the chaos that follows these interruptions. I may spin the patient around and turn the individual upside-down, thrown by his own weight, but when the patient comes down in the rubble, I will be there as a committed though world-weary companion. And as the frightening pilgrimage of life opens to the perils of the dark forces from which the patient would usually hide, I will go too, hoping that we may draw courage from one another.

Yet telling the patient all of this in advance would be futile. Most likely it would not be believed. Why should my patient trust me until we know each other? And, even if my patient would blindly follow my instructions in hope of getting what he came for, these efforts would lack the spontaneous vitality of unplanned actions arising in the fire of the moment. I am well-instructed about such matters by the Hasidic Story of the Cape:

A woman came to Rabbi Israel, the maggid of Koznitz, and told him, with many tears, that she had been married a dozen years and still had not borne a son. "What are you willing to do about it?" he asked her. She did not know what to say.

"My mother," so the maggid told her, "was aging and still had no child. Then she heard that the holy Baal Shem was stopping over in Apt in the course of a journey. She hurried to his inn and begged him to pray she might bear a son. 'What are you willing to do about it?' he asked. 'My husband is a poor bookbinder,' she replied, 'but I do have one fine thing that I shall give to the rabbi.' She went home as fast she could and fetched her good cape . . . which was carefully stowed away in a chest. But when she returned to the inn with it, she heard that the Baal Shem had already left for Mezbizh. She immediately set out after him and since she had no money to ride, she walked from town to town with her

... (cape) until she came to Mezbizh. The Baal Shem took the cape and hung it on the wall. 'It is well,' he said. My mother walked all the way back, from town to town, until she reached Apt. A year later, I was born."

"I, too," cried the woman, "will bring you a good cape of mine so that I may get a son."

"That won't work," said the maggid. "You heard the story. My mother had no story to go by."

CHAPTER FIVE

Children Know Best

A very young child is always at one with himself and is a natural part of the world. He has many questions about the world: What is it called? How does it work? Who made it? But mostly the child simply *lives* in the world, gets excited by it, tickled by it, bumped by it. The child knows that he is the one who shouts or laughs or cries, who can or cannot do things, who feels what others do and makes others feel, too.

So this child lives in the world and there is much about it that he does not understand, about which he is curious and/or scared. Yet the child somehow never steps back to ask, "What's it all about?" He seems in a state of grace when it comes to matters of the spirit. The child is totally involved in living and has neither time nor perspective in which to struggle with questions of identity or purpose or the meaning of it all.

Touch this child softly and he will smile, hurt him and he will cry, catch his openness with some glittering, bouncy bauble of life and surely he will move toward it easily and freely. You can count on the young child to respond immediately in the here and now of the moment, but never will the child stop to ask himself: "Who am I?" "What is the meaning of my life?" "How can I really be myself?" "What is my purpose in this crowded world?"

These questions are not asked until the child is an adolescent. That exciting, frightening, up/down time of transition—from being a youth to becoming an adult—is the time when spiritual questions arise. The innocence of childhood—when you live in the world as simply a part of it, and it just seems that that's the way it is, all you have to do is just be there—is lost.

All of a sudden, you are looking in on your life and there is nothing so simple about it any more. Grown-ups' answers may not be right, or, in any case, may not be relevant to you. "Let me look at myself," you say. "Let me see how I feel. Let me try to understand so that I can live the kind of life that will make sense to me, that will make me feel best about who I am in the world, and about what my place is in it." Adolescence is a time to search for your own answers.

This spiritual seeking does not begin until adolescence. Perhaps that is why spiritual guides do not appear in tales for young children. Instead we usually find magic helpers who grant the wishes of the good characters and punish the naughty ones. Wish-granting and rescuing helpers (such as the Fairy Godmother in "Cinderella" and the Woodsman in "Little Red Riding Hood") rarely require any self-understanding of the hero (with whom the child identifies).

Perhaps it is this very unselfconscious simplicity, so appropriate to the world of the young child, that is so boring to the dutiful adult who repeatedly reads or tells the tales to the child. I think of few exceptions, few tales with characters whom children like and yet whose problems touch familiar chords in the adult who is reading the story. It is only in such children's tales as these that the characters get into trouble because of the way in which they approach life rather than because of the bad witch who casts a spell on them. And it is only in such children's tales as these that we find a helper, healer, or guide who might serve as a metaphor for a psychotherapist. The two examples which we will examine are the Winnie-the-Pooh stories by A. A. Milne and *The Wizard of Oz* by L. Frank Baum.

THE WISE FRIEND

The Winnie-the-Pooh tales originated as stories made up by Alan Alexander Milne to please his son Christopher Robin

Milne. Christopher, himself, was the Wise Friend in the stories. The other characters were his very own stuffed animals, delightfully brought to life by his father's loving imagination.

Each of the characters has a very definite personality, typically one that embodies common human foibles. The central character, Winnie-the-Pooh, is "a Bear of Very Little Brain," who does not think things out clearly. He avoids unpleasant realities for as long as he can. Instead he concentrates on whether it isn't "Time for a Little Something" (such as a lick of honey or condensed milk on some bread).

On the other hand, Eeyore, the Old Gray Donkey, spends too much time thinking about all the terrible things that might befall him. He tries to figure them out in advance and hardly ever has any fun. In his gloomy way, he is always asking himself, "Why?" and "Wherefore?" and "Inasmuch as which?" He is so full of doubts that it sometimes seems to him that he has not felt anything else for a long time.

Another character, Rabbit, is often imposed upon by his "Friends and Relations" because he is too polite to say no. Tigger, the bouncy young tiger, is just the opposite. He is destructively impatient in his search for personal satisfaction. In order "to find out what Tiggers like," he is forever bowling over the other characters in the stories. This aggressive behavior is especially hard on Piglet, who is afraid of almost everything. Of course, Piglet pretends that he is not upset, as when, "to show that he hadn't been frightened, he jumped up and down once or twice in an exercising sort of way."[1]

These very personality characteristics, these all-too-human hang-ups, often get these characters into trouble. And when in trouble, they usually turn to their Wise Friend, Christopher Robin, for help. This wise friend is a boy who is patient, understanding, and loving. And what is more, Christopher Robin has a perspective that the others sadly lack. He is often the only one who looks at things as they are.

For instance, there was the time when Winnie-the-Pooh was wandering, perhaps hoping to find a Little Something, when he came upon some paw marks. Pooh got Piglet to join him (to show that he wasn't frightened). Piglet went along because he was sure it would turn out to be a harmless Woozle. Together they went round and round a large tree tracking what might "turn out to be Hostile Animals." But as this pair of mighty hunters circled the tree again and again, more and more tracks of Woozles appeared. At last, they saw their Wise Friend, Christopher Robin, perched high up above them in the branches of a big oak tree. He came down to talk to them about their problem:

> "Silly old Bear," he said, "what *were* you doing?" First you went round the . . . [tree] twice by yourself, and then Piglet ran after you and you went round again together, and then you were just going round a fourth time—"
>
> "Wait a moment," said Winnie-the-Pooh, holding up his paw.
>
> He sat down and thought, in the most thoughtful way he could think. Then he lifted his paw into one of the tracks . . . and then he scratched his nose twice and stood up.
>
> "Yes," said Winnie-the-Pooh.
>
> "I see now," said Winnie-the-Pooh.
>
> "I have been Foolish and Deluded," said he, "and I am a Bear of No Brain at All."
>
> "You're the Best Bear in All the World," said Christopher Robin soothingly.[2]

In this case, the Wise Friend's perspective and reassurance were enough. In other cases, this good counsel is effective only if the character who is in trouble is willing to pay the price for his foolishness.

Such another case occurred the time that Winnie-the-Pooh dropped in at Rabbit's hole unannounced, in hope of finding a Little Something. Rabbit was, of course, too polite to turn Pooh down; he was too polite even to stop Pooh while Pooh ate every bit of honey, condensed milk, and bread in Rabbit's hole. At last, when there was nothing more to eat, Pooh attempted to leave. I say "attempted" because by now Pooh was so stuffed that he could only get halfway through the entrance to Rabbit's hole. And there, halfway through, Pooh was stuck until Christopher Robin, his Wise Friend, came along. It was clear that Pooh would have to remain stuck for a week before he would be thin enough to get free again.

"A week!" said Pooh gloomily. *"What about meals?"*

"I'm afraid no meals," said Christopher Robin, "because of getting thin quicker. But we *will* read to you."

Bear began to sigh, and then found he couldn't because he was so tightly stuck; and a tear rolled down his eye, as he said:

"Then would you read a Sustaining Book, such as would help and comfort a Wedged Bear in Great Tightness?"[3]

And, of course, Christopher Robin did just exactly that for a whole week, as "Bear felt himself getting slenderer and slenderer." Some helpers feel that even if the troubled person has to live out his own struggle in order to get out of that trouble, the helper can offer something to sustain the troubled person during the ordeal. As we shall come to see, in the case of the Wonderful Wizard, some helpers do not feel this way at all.

THE WONDERFUL WIZARD

Therapist: I am Oz, the Great and Terrible. Who are you, and why do you seek me?

Patient: I am Dorothy, the Small and Meek. I have come to you for help. I am lost out here in this world, and I want you to get me back to Kansas, where I will be safe and comfortable.

Therapist: Why should I do this for you?

Patient: Because you are strong and I am weak, because you are a great Wizard and I am only a helpless little girl.

Therapist: But you were strong enough to kill the Wicked Witch of the East.

Patient: That just happened. I could not help it.

Therapist: Well, I will give you my answer. You have no right to expect me to send you back to Kansas unless you do something for me in return. In this country everyone must pay for everything he gets. If you wish me to use my magic power to send you home again, you must do something for me first. Help me and I will help you.

Patient: I will do anything you ask, anything. Only tell me. What must I do?

Therapist: Kill the Wicked Witch of the West.

Patient: No, that I cannot, will not do.

Most readers will recognize this bit of dialogue as being more or less the way it appeared in *The Wizard of Oz*,[4] although I have recast it as an initial exchange between therapist and patient. It was in 1900 that L. Frank Baum, self-appointed royal Historian of Oz, published the first of his chronicles. He wrote it as the beginning of a series of modern wonder tales. But unlike the writers of earlier stories, he hoped to eliminate "all the horrible and bloodcurdling incidents devised by their authors to point a fearsome moral to each tale."

Baum wrote, in part, as an expression of his own dissatisfaction with Victorian ideas of building character through punishment, stern lectures, and inner struggles for self-control, sacrifice, and self-denial. To solve our problems, he visualized instead the possibility of personal growth through acceptance of ourselves, with humor if need be, and through a central role in a loving relationship. And, too, he believed that all of this could be accomplished only by learning that the powerful other, the authority, the Wizard to whom we look for help, is himself only another struggling human being.

The continued success of this book and of the motion picture made from it—they perpetually reengage us with delight in the characters' adventures—is testimony to the compelling quality of Baum's vision. In all of this I see some themes that are at the core of my own sort of psychotherapy. I would like, therefore, to reexamine some aspects of *The Wizard of Oz* as a psychotherapeutic tale.

In the original story, Dorothy, the young heroine of the tale, is an orphan who has come to live with foster parents, Aunt Em and Uncle Henry. Their home is dull and gray, as is everything else in the sunbaked, unyielding land of Kansas, U.S.A. Aunt Em is described as an unsmiling sober woman, thin and gaunt, who, when Dorothy first came, was so startled by the girl's laughter that it would cause her to scream and press her hand upon her heart. Uncle Henry is a man who never laughed, looked stern and solemn, and rarely spoke. It was only Dorothy's dog Toto and her good heart that made her laugh and saved her from growing as gray as her surroundings.

Early in the story, Dorothy is separated by a cyclone from her foster family and from the world of familiarly unhappy surroundings. The storm whisks her and Toto, together with their house, away from the plains of Kansas, U.S.A., off to the bewildering land of Oz. It is this crisis of being uprooted, flooded with fantasy, and no longer in touch with the familiar misery of home that leads Dorothy to seek the help of the Wizard of Oz in his great palace in Emerald City. Her house, it seems, had landed on the Wicked Witch of the East and killed her. Dorothy, of course, points out that this is in no way her fault. In fact, Aunt Em had told her that there were no witches living anyway. The Good Witch of the North (a good mother, at last) is of more help. She has Dorothy put on the ruby slippers of the dead witch and refers her to the Wizard for treatment of her problems.

And so, like many patients. Dorothy seeks treatment, not out of having some perspective on her long unhappy family life, but rather in the midst of a crisis of the moment that separates her from her family or from her usual ways of handling things at home. It is so often not chronic unhappiness, but rather present confusion and situational distress that lead people to the office of the psychotherapist. All Dorothy wants is to go back home to the known safety of her unsatisfactory family life, rather than tolerate the promise of her new and unfamiliar world. *She prefers the security of misery to the misery of insecurity.*

On the way to Emerald City she meets other distressed creatures who need psychotherapy but do not know it is available until they meet Dorothy. They are, of course, the Scarecrow, the Tin Woodman, and the Cowardly Lion. The Scarecrow's problem is that he has no brains at all. Dorothy finds him perched on a stick in a cornfield, harassed by crows. He is the inadequate man, who acts foolishly and is sure that his foolishness is no fault of his own—he simply lacks what he needs to behave competently and wisely. In the meanwhile, people must not expect too much of him, but must protect him from fire because he is stuffed with straw.

Next Dorothy comes upon the Tin Woodman standing in the woods with uplifted ax in his hands, rusted so badly that he cannot move. His problem is that though he seems very polite, he has no heart. He once was a man of flesh and blood, but was hurt so often that he gradually had all the parts of his body replaced with tin. And, alas, the heart was left out. He, too, is not responsible for this unfortunate state of affairs. If only someone would do something for him, he might be able to really care about people instead of merely appearing to be polite. His problem with rust requires that other people be around to oil him up, or he just won't be able to function.

The third companion startles them in the woods. It is the Cowardly Lion, who menaces them with unwarranted mock ferocity but all too quickly reveals that he is nothing but a big coward. Although he has brains and heart and home, he lacks courage. Therefore, he cannot be expected to follow through with boldness, to risk himself, to act like a man—or rather like a lion. He roars to scare others off, but if they stay to challenge, he shows his cowardice. "But how can I help it?" he pleads and then tells Dorothy that, now that she knows this, she must be careful not to frighten him.

When all four know one another's problems, they set out for the therapist's office on a joint venture that you might expect to give them some sense of empathy and genuine consideration for one another. Instead, after their mutual disclosures, each mutters self-centeredly to himself.

The Scarecrow: "All the same, I shall ask for brains instead of a heart; for a fool would not know what to do with a heart if he had one."

The Tin Woodman: "I shall take the heart, for brains do not make one happy, and happiness is the best thing in the world."

The Cowardly Lion: "What they each want is certainly less important than courage."

And finally there was good sweet little Dorothy; if only she could get back home, she really wouldn't care whether or not the others got what they wanted.

Apparently the really important thing is to get one's own way.

When at last they arrive at the Palace in Emerald City, the Wizard does individual intake interviews with each of them. And as it is with new patients, each sees him very differently from the others. He appears variously to them as a lovely winged lady on a throne, an enormous head, a ball of fire, and a most terrible monster. Each approaches him as Dorothy did: "I am Dorothy, the Small and Meek. I have come to you for help. . . ." Each is frightened and helpless. Somehow this entitles each one to special help and consideration which the Wizard absolutely must give, simply because he is adequate and strong. The Wizard, good therapist that he is, quickly comes across as a person who has his own needs. In therapy country, people must pay for what they get, meaning, these poor helpless patients must give something of themselves if they wish to get something for themselves.

The Wizard assigns them the task of killing the Wicked Witch of the West. They would like the Wizard to destroy the bad mother for them, but no matter how great and powerful a father he seems, he cannot do for them what they must do for themselves. He cannot even tell them how to go about their task. Each patient tries to "cop out" in his own way. Dorothy has already "accidentally" killed the Wicked Witch of the East, but this time she must kill willingly and not by accident or without responsibility. She is reluctant because she cannot be forceful on purpose. Scarecrow says he will not be able to help because he is a fool; Tin Woodman because he does not have the heart for it; and Cowardly Lion because he is too fearful. In order to help them, however, the Wizard will not let them off the hook.

So, reluctantly, they set off to slay the Wicked Witch of the West. In the course of this adventure, in spite of themselves, they are caught up in their task and grow to have genuine concern for one another—so much so, that the Scarecrow makes wise decisions, the Tin Woodman acts out of loyalty, and the Cowardly Lion performs bravely. Even Dorothy learns to be happy for her friends and their achievements, even when she fears she may never achieve her own desires.

This task assigned by the Wizard is a kind of teaching by indirection. As in psychotherapy, he insists they will get nowhere if they simply continue to bewail their fates and to insist stubbornly that because they have troubles, *he* must solve their problems magically (or at least be terribly sympathetic). Instead the Wizard directs their attentions elsewhere.

In individual therapy we may get the patient to focus on his past history. In group therapy, we may encourage the patient's curiosity about the group process. Some of what occurs as the patient reluctantly takes on these tasks is that the individual begins to lose himself when he gives himself over to the assigned work. As the patient is unhooked from his willful, self-sorry demand for relief right now, a new possibility arises: the patient now begins to experience the therapist and the other patients as real people with selves of their own—people who have meaning who can therefore be meaningful to him, and who can ultimately put him in touch with the meaning of his own life.

Once our adventurers have accomplished what they first insisted they could not possibly do—that is, slay the Witch—they return to the Wizard, impatient for their rewards. They have not yet realized that they already possess these rewards. In the course of asserting themselves at the Wizard's palace, they learn that he is not a Wizard at all—he is "just a common man," or worse, a humbug! When he is challenged, it turns out that he has problems of his own. Disillusioned, Dorothy tells him, "I think you are a very bad man." "Oh, no, my dear," he answers, "I'm really a very good man, though I'm a very bad Wizard, I must admit."

The Wizard then tries to help them understand the solutions at which they have already arrived. For Scarecrow, it was not a problem of lacking brains, but of avoiding the experiences that would yield knowledge. Now that he would risk being wrong, he could sometimes act wisely. So too with the Tin Woodman: it was not a heart he lacked, but rather a willingness to bear unhappiness. And, of course, Cowardly Lion needed not courage, but the confidence to know that he could face danger even when he was terribly afraid. Then Baum, with sympathetic tolerance for human foibles, has each patient insist that the Wizard confirm the individual accomplishment with an external token. In one version, the Wizard presents Scarecrow with a diploma, gives Tin Woodman a solid gold watch for loyal service, and awards the lion a medal for bravery.

As for Dorothy, she learns that all she had to do to get home was to use the ruby slippers she wore. She needed only to knock the heels together three times and the shoes would carry her wherever she wished to go. That is, she learned that she had the power to go wherever she wanted and to make changes in her life if only she was willing to take the responsibility of recognizing and using that power.

Of course, the Wizard could have told them all this at the beginning of treatment, but they never would have believed him. How could they have accepted that their demands from others were human qualities that they already possessed? The insights are too simple to be grasped, too obvious to see, and can only be had when a person stops demanding them from the powerful Wizard/Parent who is supposed to take care of him. The patient must give up the internal struggle and become involved with another and with what comes between them.

Baum revitalized old lessons which must be learned again and again: wisdom involves risk of being wrong or foolish; love and tenderness requires a willingness to bear unhappiness; courage is the confidence to face danger despite fear; freedom and power require only a willingness to recognize their existence and to face their consequences. We can find ourselves only when we are willing to risk losing ourselves to another, to the moment, to a quest; *love is the bridge.*

But last of all, alas, there are no Wizards! And yet, as a psychotherapist, I am sometimes tempted to join the Wonderful Wizard of Oz in saying, "But how can I help being a humbug, when all these people make me do things that everybody knows can't be done?"

CHAPTER SIX

Yesterday's Fiction Is Tomorrow's Science

Among science fiction enthusiasts, there is a saying: "Science fiction of today, Science of tomorrow." Space travel is perhaps the most dramatic instance of such dreams which have come true. But the projections of science fiction writers have not been restricted to plausible extensions of science and technology. In some instances, the science fiction tale involves an attempt to help us to see where we might be headed in other terms. The tools and weapons of contemporary man, and also his attitudes and social institutions, may yet lead him toward heaven or into the depths of hell. In some of the science fiction writings we can discover projections of future helpers, healers, and guides, as well as prefigures of their deadly counterparts. One such sinister guru is the Director of Hatcheries and Conditioning.

THE DIRECTOR OF HATCHERIES AND CONDITIONING

Every utopia has its price. Is it ever less than exorbitant? This question was examined by Aldous Huxley in his science fiction classic, *Brave New World*. Written in 1932, this novel was an attempt to serve as an early, and as yet unheeded, warning. Earlier than most, Huxley was aware of some of the dangers of twentieth-century man's thrust toward a mushrooming technology, of the unevenly distributed fruits of overproduction, and of the gluttonous consumption of luxuries.

He realized that Western man grasped at the promise of Science as the yearned-for panacea, as the possibility of turning civilization into a latter-day Eden. Of course, in order for this society to realize its fullest technological expansion rapidly enough to enjoy its fruits, those who were less comfortable would have to endure further hardships. But then that's the only way *they* know how to live.

Indeed, everyone might have to endure certain individual sacrifices for the good of mankind. In the long run, it would certainly be best for humanity if Science and State could somehow merge into a benevolent "technocracy." The necessary enlightened controls would be built into the system. Individual rights would be less of an issue. People could be guided to do what was best for them (and for everyone else). At last, all could know the coming of a brave new world, a utopia born of man's technological know-how that served everyone's needs as they should best be served.

The brave new world is a time and place in which spiritual problems are solved in advance, by the grace of governmental planning and control, in the form of scientific programming and prevention. The new guru—the helper, healer, and guide of the new world—is the technocratic state personified by the Director of Hatcheries and Conditioning—the D.H.C. The agency which the D.H.C. directs is the major instrument of social stability on a planet whose one-world motto has become: "Community, Identity, Stability."

The predestining and conditioning of infants begins before birth, though the D.H.C. complains that "you can't really do any useful conditioning till the fetuses have lost their tails." In this new scientific era, of course, the embryos no longer need to develop in the uterus. Instead, they are grown in specialized scientific equipment at the Hatchery. In that way, their chemical environment is varied so that babies are "decanted," already predestined for one of the social castes (designated Alpha, Beta, Gamma, etc.).

Each baby at birth (or when "decanted") ideally is suited biologically for a social role (ranging from moronic servant to sensitive aristocrat). It only remains then for the D.H.C. to condition the baby to be suited psychologically for this role in life. To accomplish this, the D.H.C. has caste-segregated infant nurseries set up as Neo-Pavlovian Conditioning Rooms.

For example, in a Delta infant nursery, khaki-clad infants are prepared for simple mechanical work. Flowers and colorful books are put on the floor. These eight-month infants crawl eagerly toward them. The D.H.C. gives a signal and the head nurse pulls down a little lever. Suddenly, the quiet room gives way to shrill sirens and loud alarm bells. The children scream in terror. Now the D.H.C. signals for the electrified grid in the floor to be turned on; this shocks the children into pain and panic, "to rub in the lesson."

These Delta children will no longer approach books and flowers. A lack of books means no ideas to cause discontentment with their mechanical destinies. A lack of flowers means an avoidance of the economic problems of the past when such masses flocked to the country. These children will grow up in the city and will consume all of the manufactured items necessary in order to support the State's economy. Consumption of goods is the mainstay of this technocracy. If something wears out, it is thrown away, for "ending is better than mending." This and other slogans constitute the heart of the moral education of the people of this brave new world. These homilies are taught by tape recordings played while the children sleep. This sleep-teaching, or *hypnopaedia,* instills all that is needed, from basic slogans like, "Everyone belongs to everyone else," to the specific teachings about caste and consumption.

The needs and desires of the people are manipulated and turned toward those goals which the State finds are most useful to offer—useful in terms of the State's self-perpetuation. Frustration is held to a minimum so that no one is "compelled to live through a long time-interval between the consciousness of a desire and its fulfillment."[1] Any moment of dissatisfaction that slips through the network of programmed "happiness" is obliterated by *soma,* the perfect drug. (It is "euphoric, narcotic, pleasantly hallucinant," and government-sponsored.) Soma has "all the advantages of Christianity and alcohol" without any of the defects. If the D.H.C.'s work has not solved all problems for all time, a dose of soma provides a holiday from reality whenever needed. Remember, "One cubic centimeter cures ten gloomy sentiments."[2]

THE MINISTER OF LOVE

Huxley's Director of Hatcheries and Conditioning programs each child to be a happy consumer. He preconditions each of his wards to fit into the role that will serve best to perpetuate progress in the technological society. In the process, the D.H.C. sets up each citizen's needs so that this brave new world will satisfy without needless frustration. The price of this contentment is the loss of individual freedom and self-determination.

George Orwell's science fiction novel, *Nineteen Eighty-four,* is another utopian nightmare. Huxley warned of the dangers into which the idealization of Science may lead us; Orwell tells us that we must beware of giving the State a great deal of power in the misguided hope that it will take care of us. He extends in fantasy that which he sees as the already inherent totalitarian menace: the danger that arises when those who run the government try to control the thinking of a citizenry whom they insist do not know what is good for them.

Winston, Orwell's hero, lives in the year 1984, in the midst of such frightening benevolence. There are enormous posters everywhere of the leader's face, with eyes that seem to follow you when you move. The caption on each poster reads:

BIG BROTHER IS WATCHING YOU

There is no escape. Even at home, there is a compulsory tele-screen, a sort of "improved" TV which transmits propaganda and watches the viewer at the same time. It cannot be shut off. Winston is one of the fortunate elite, a Party member, who helps the State run this society. He works in the Ministry of Truth, the part of government which controls news, education, entertainment, and fine arts. His job in the Records Department is to rewrite old speeches and news releases. This "reconstruction of the past" allows the State to deal with new developments without running the risk of ever being wrong.

For instance, one day there is a news release that tells of great military victories, and as usual it is followed by a demand for greater sacrifices. In this case, the individual chocolate ration is reduced from thirty to twenty grams per week. A few days later, another news release tells of "spontaneous demonstrations" which have taken place to thank Big Brother for *raising* the chocolate ration to twenty grams per week. Soon afterward Winston is instructed to rewrite one of Big Brother's earlier speeches so that it appears that Big Brother predicted this raising of the chocolate ration.

Despite Winston's favored position, he is still subject to telescreen scrutiny and must participate in the compulsory, scheduled, ritual vilifications of "enemies of the State" during Hate Week. Physical training is required in order for him to maintain the stamina to serve, and he must maintain willing acceptance of this, as of all his other obligations to the State. The eyes and ears of the Thought Police (and of patriotic citizens) make it necessary for him to watch what he says lest he be prosecuted for a thoughtcrime. Even his facial expressions are monitored, so a grimace (when a smile is demanded) may result in prosecution for a facecrime. He knows that at any time he can be "vaporized." If this happens, the Thought Police will drag him off into the night, and if it is advantageous to the State, all record of his existence on earth will be expunged along with his disappearance.

Nonetheless, Winston has a residual inclination to think for himself, supported by the awareness of contradictions provided by his position with the Records Department. The catalyst in this unstable mixture is a woman named Julia. Though she wears the traditional narrow scarlet waist sash, the emblem of the Junior Anti-Sex League, Julia has an enthusiastic commitment to eroticism. It so happens that the State is involved in eradicating the sexual urge, along with other pleasures which compete with the desire to serve. Thus, Winston and Julia's lovemaking becomes an act of political defiance.

Winston increasingly becomes committed to political freedom. No longer will he accept the Party slogans:

WAR IS PEACE
FREEDOM IS SLAVERY
IGNORANCE IS STRENGTH

He now is puzzled by the Doublethink, which previously had allowed him to believe that a thing could be true and untrue, depending on how it related to the State. He goes so far as to remember and talk about what had gone on in the past, before it was reconstructed.

At last his political disaffection comes to the attention of the Thought Police. He ends up deep in the cellars of the Ministry of Love. In Orwell's 1984, it is no longer impossible for the branch of government that maintains law and order to be a windowless, barricaded, well-guarded, steel-doored fortress, a dreaded place called the Ministry of Love. In this totalitarian age, the healer of the soul is a sadistic agent of the State, risen to a position of refined cruelty—the Minister of Love.

Winston's encounter with O'Brien, the Minister of Love, consists of torture, for his own good. Winston is mad enough to question the dictates of Big Brother, and now O'Brien must "cure" him. The first part of the cure involves conditioning his thoughts with electrically induced, controlled pain. The Minister of Love tells Winston:

> You know perfectly well what is the matter with you. You have known it for years though you have fought against the knowledge. You are mentally deranged. You suffer from a defective memory. You are unable to remember real events, and you persuade yourself that you remember other events which never happened. Fortunately, it is curable. . . .[3]

In order to "cure" Winston, the Minister of Love must change his thinking, his perception, his memory. The emphasis on memory is crucial. This is made clear in the Party slogan:

WHO CONTROLS THE PAST CONTROLS THE FUTURE
WHO CONTROLS THE PRESENT CONTROLS THE PAST

Memories which do not fit within the State's reconstruction of history are "delusions." Experiences which do not concur are "hallucinations."

The Minister of Love is not interested in merely changing Winston's behavior. He seeks the abject submission of Winston's sorrow for what he has done and renewed love for Big Brother. Confession and punishment are not the goals. It is known that everything else follows if the freedom is granted to say that two plus two make five. O'Brien knows that Winston must undergo "an act of self-destruction," that he must "humble himself" before he can become sane. And so the Minister of Love subjects him to a scientifically systematic program of torture aimed at making him "see" five fingers (because the Party says there are five) when there are really only four.

Finally, after many nightmarish days, Winston has "been kicked and flogged and insulted . . . screamed with pain [and] rolled on the floor in . . . [his] own blood and vomit."[4] Still, he has not been sufficiently degraded. The Minister of Love warns: "We shall squeeze you empty and then we shall fill you with ourselves."[5]

Only one final degradation is needed—that Winston betray Julia, not only in words but in his very heart.

In order to accomplish this, the Minister of Love must resort to the final step, Room 101. Room 101 contains "the worst thing in the world." For each citizen its contents are different. For Winston, Room 101 contains rats. He cannot even think about rats without feeling terrified. Now he faces a cage from which rats will be released to attack his face. He screams, "Do it to Julia! Not me."

He has been cured completely by the Minister of Love. He is thoroughly penitent and filled with gratitude toward Big

Brother for his redemption. In his joy and renewal, he can no longer remember that while he was still mad, the Minister of Love had told him, "If you want a picture of the future, imagine a boot stamping on a human face—forever."[6]

THE PLANETARY EXPLORATION AND SETTLEMENT BOARD

Not all science fiction predicts so nightmarish a future. Some tales describe promise, while others merely explore the future with a neutral curiosity. In Robert Sheckley's story "The Minimum Man," the hero is an inadequate fellow who would be a completely recognizable figure in our own time. In Sheckley's world of the future, the hero receives therapy by accident, as an unforeseen outgrowth of the exploration of space. A Planetary Exploration and Settlement Board serves as the planner of the therapeutic milieu and a Robot serves as an alter ego.

Our hero, Anton Percerveral, is thirty-four years old and is about to commit suicide. He always makes mistakes; no accident or minor illness evades him; he loses whatever is small enough to misplace and breaks those larger things. Job after job is lost and satisfactory friendships are impossible to come by. He has undergone Analysis, Hypnotic Suggestion, Hypnotic Hypersuggestion, and Countersuggestion Removal. No form of treatment is beyond the impact of his inadequacy.

His suicide attempt is similarly unsuccessful: it is interrupted by a telegram from the Planetary Exploration and Settlement Board. He is offered a job as an Extraterrestrial Explorer, a job for which he earlier had been turned down. He protests to the Planetary Board that this must be an error. Haskell, the representative of the Planetary Board, explains that in the early days they chose only the most competent men as explorers, men who could survive wherever human survival was possible. But now, overpopulation created great demand for colonization of land in which even the most ordinary men could survive. So, the qualifications for explorers were changed. Now, instead of using optimal-survival explorers, they sought minimum-survival men, such as Anton Percerveral. Such men are contacted when their hopes run out, when suicide seems imminent.

Anton, seeing that the job is no more dangerous than suicide, decides to take the job. He is sent to the unexplored planet of Theta, with a Robot as an assistant. Soon enough he finds that much of his equipment either malfunctions, breaks, or wears out. He contacts Haskell, who tells him that these failures are control elements for maintaining minimal survival conditions.

Anton reacts to these built-in foul-ups (which, for once in his life, are not of his making) by learning to repair, take care of, and properly use all of the equipment. However, his newly developing survival talents are counteracted by the growing destructiveness of the Robot. Anton also learns from Haskell that the Robot is a flexible quality control mechanism for maintaining the minimal survival conditions. As Anton becomes more skillful and less accident-prone, the Robot's behavior deteriorates. As times goes on, Anton

> learned how to live with the Robot.... The Robot now seemed the embodiment of that other, darker side of himself, the inept and accident-prone Percerveral.... The Robot came to represent his own destructive urges cut loose from the life impulse and allowed to run rampant. Percerveral worked, and his neurosis stalked behind him, eternally destructive, yet—in the manner of neurosis—protective of itself.[7]

With the help of some of the mole-like inhabitants of Theta, Anton buries the Robot underground and then spends his own time improving his survival skills. At last he feels he has become adequate and that he is ready to declare Theta safe for the survival of other ordinary men. In the name of the Planetary Board, Haskell warns that the Robot, that personification of Anton's neurosis, may have been only temporarily set aside and not yet fully destroyed.

Haskell is right. With the aid of self-repair units, the Robot reappears, more destructive than ever. Anton prepares a series of traps for the Robot, but none of them work, for

> how can a man trick the trickiest part of himself? The right hand always finds out what the left hand is doing, and the cleverest of devices never fools the supreme fooler for long.[8]

At last Anton realizes that his methods are wrong. He sees that "the way to freedom is not through deception." He must give up trying to conquer the Robot and concentrate on overcoming his kinship with it. When it is no longer *his* neurosis, but simply *a* neurosis, it will lose its power over him.

Filled with new confidence, with enthusiasm, with laughter, Anton simply trusts himself and moves with whatever feels right. The clumsy Robot is thrown by its own weight and Anton is free at last. His work is done. Haskell arrives on Theta as a representative of the Planetary Board in the colony ship, *Cuchulain*.

Haskell tells Anton he was successful. The planet is ready for colonization, and he may remain there for his many rewards. Anton wants to go to explore another planet, but Haskell points out that he no longer qualifies as a minimum-survival person. Anton turns away in disappointment, stumbles, spills some ink, trips, and bangs his head. But Haskell is not to be fooled. Anton must live up to his newfound adequacy.

In this story, scientific developments for curing neurosis are mentioned, but they all fail when applied to Anton. Successful therapy comes to Anton in the form of the Planetary Board, those who encourage exploration and risk-taking. The Planetary Board sets the scene but is unconcerned with a cure for Anton. The Planetary Board knows that Anton must face the destructive forces himself (in the form of the Robot) and not just bury them.

In this story, the Machine represents the neurosis. In Ray Bradbury's "The Lost City of Mars," the Machine is the therapist.

THE MACHINE

Bradbury writes about a chronically unhappy married couple who wander through an aging, abandoned city on the red planet of Mars. These people, who trudge along the empty streets past the cracked windows of empty shops, are poet Harpwell and his wife Megeen.

They battle, as they always do. He is calculatingly obscene, and she is dependably righteous and condemning. She sums up her complaints about him: "The whole thing is ... you only came along so you could lay hands on the nearest woman and spray her ears with bad breath and worse poetry."[9] To all of this, he can only answer, "Ah, God, I've curdled inside. Shut up, woman," and lapse into more obscenity. The interplanetary Harpwells are a latter-day Dylan and Caitlin Thomas.

At last, the poet runs off in a rage and escapes into an abandoned building, the doors of which slam and lock behind him. Within the building, Harpwell finds himself in a great domed room which houses a large, complicated Machine with a sort of a driver's seat, complete with steering wheel, dials, and switches. Never able to leave anything alone, the poet seats himself at the wheel, flips a switch, and grabs onto the steering wheel tightly as the great Machine seems to shiver, bolt, and dash ahead.

Suddenly Harpwell finds himself in a car, racing down a highway at ninety miles an hour. Coming toward him at the same deadly speed is another car, maneuvering reciprocally in order to obviate his every attempt to avoid a head-on collision. There is no brake, no stopping the crash. He screams! There is a terrible collision, the tearing apart of metal, the explosion, and the broken torch it all became. Harpwell lay dead—but only for a while.

He finds himself not only alive again and once more seated at the controls of the Machine, but interested, fascinated, indeed, exhilarated. For a moment he thinks of Megeen and wishes she were there to see it all, but only for a moment. Again he flips switches and tinkers with dials, seeking another "diversion." This time it is the cars all over again, only much faster. Again the crash, the dying, the reviving only to feel even more alive. It is "queer beyond queerness."

Again and again, he dials and switches on the violence, the dying, and the reviving. Faster and faster, he sets the pace. Eventually, for the cars, he substitutes locomotives approaching on the same track, ramming jets, missiles screaming through space toward each other.

Bit by bit he begins to see what the Machine is all about:

> I begin to know what this is used for; for such as me, the poor wandering idiots of the world, confused and sore, put upon by mothers as soon as dropped from wombs, insulted with Christian guilt, and gone mad from the need of destruction and collecting a pittance of hurt here and scar tissue there, and a larger portable wife grievance. . . . We do want to die, we want to be killed, and here's the very thing for it, in convenient quick pay! So pay it out, machine, dole it out. . . .[10]

Half an hour later, he is sitting at the Machine, beginning to laugh. He is happy in a way so new and so promising that he never need drink again. He has been so hurt and punished that he never need be involved in another self-destructive act for the rest of his life. His guilt has been paid for. His need to be destroyed has been satisfied at last.

Happy, and grateful too, he finds his way out of the building. Megeen is outside, ready to begin her screaming once more. But the poet is free, "off the Christian hook." He no longer needs the mental punishment of life with Megeen; he wanders off laughing joyously. Bewildered, his abandoned wife wanders into the building which houses the Machine. Sniffing and scowling, she seeks a new opponent. The doors close behind her.

CHAPTER SEVEN

Foolish Heroes and Wise Villains

And the soul,
if she is to know herself,
must look
into the soul:
the stranger and the enemy, we saw him in the mirror.[1]

"Beauty and the Beast"[2] is a lovely fairy-tale variant on the perennial human theme of the merging of opposites. Sometimes its message is diluted to the shallow sentimentalization that "a true heart is better than either good looks or clever brains." But the intuitive response of my own dark soul tells me that its lasting truth has to do instead with each Innocent's need to lay claim to the Beast within himself.

Think back over the years to the time when you believed all the tales of wonder which you now are too rational and mature to appreciate. Can you recall that Beauty was the youngest and most beautiful child of a once-very-rich merchant who had six children, three boys and three girls? The other daughters were vain, while Beauty was the innocent. The other daughters sought husbands but she thought herself too young to marry and instead chose to live devotedly with her father. When the merchant lost his fortune the family had to move to a small cottage in the country. Of all the children, only Beauty could accept her fate with humility and devotion. She worked hard without complaining while the others indulged themselves with breakfast in bed. Occasionally when fortune arrived, Beauty asked for nothing for herself while the others made outrageous demands. When the father insisted upon something for Beauty, she said she would be happy with a single rose.

On his way back from his journey the father got presents for each of his children, but since it was midwinter he couldn't find a rose for Beauty. As he wandered through the dark night, cold and hungry, he came upon a great house. No one was at home. He entered, ate, and slept. He hoped the master of the house would forgive him. When he awoke late in the morning, he found a handsome new suit of clothes to replace his own torn, soiled garments. He thought he was in the home of a good fairy who was taking care of him.

After breakfast he went into the garden and picked a bunch of roses to carry home to Beauty. Just then he heard a loud noise and saw a beast come toward him, a beast so frightening that the man almost fainted with fear. The Beast was furious: the man had rewarded his hospitality by stealing his roses. The Beast told him that he would soon die for this transgression. The merchant begged for mercy and explained why he would gather a rose for Beauty at any cost. The Beast told the merchant he would be freed if one of his daughters was sent to replace him. If not, then the man must return in three months to be killed. The merchant pretended—with a solemn promise—to accept the Beast's terms so he could return home and see his children once more. The Beast agreed and gave him many lovely things to take home to his family.

When the merchant returned, he told his children of his plight. The other daughters blamed Beauty for their father's troubles. But Beauty said, "It is not necessary that my father die. I will give myself up to the Beast and prove my love for the best of fathers." The brothers objected and said they would go and search for the monster. The father did not want any of the children to suffer and said he would go back and give himself up to the Beast. But Beauty stubbornly argued her love and insisted that she go. After three months, Beauty prepared for her trip to the Beast's castle. The other daughters pretended to be upset, but Beauty herself went willingly.

When Beauty and her father arrived at the castle, they were

fed. (Beauty suspected the Beast wanted to fatten her up before he ate her up.) The Beast appeared and asked Beauty if she had come of her own accord. When she replied that she had, he answered, "Then you are a good girl and I am very much obliged to you." Beauty and her father were bewildered. The merchant left sadly and Beauty went to her room to sleep. During the night, Beauty dreamed that a lady came to her, and said, "I am very pleased, Beauty, that you have been willing to give your life to save that of your father. Do not be afraid; you shall not go without a reward." Beauty was amazed to find that the Beast had done what he could to make her accommodations lovely and pleasant; now she knew he did not want to hurt her. As they got to know each other, Beauty admitted that the Beast was very ugly, but she also knew that he was very kind. The beast admitted his ugliness and also claimed to be stupid, but Beauty told him that stupid people are never aware of their own stupidity.

Gradually, Beauty became so responsive to the Beast's kindness that she began to forget how ugly he was. At one point the monster said, "There is many a monster with the form of a man. It is the better of the two to have the heart of a man and form of a monster." Eventually the Beast asked Beauty if she would marry him. She was frightened but since she was always truthful she said, "No." He was sad but not angry. Over the months her sympathy and affection for the Beast grew. Eventually she looked forward to the time they spent together. The only thing that bothered her, besides missing her father, was that the Beast again and again asked if she would marry him. After a while, she asked the Beast if she might go home to visit her father. She felt that his heart must be breaking with grief over their separation. The Beast said she could go, but if she stayed away he himself would surely die of sorrow. Beauty assured him that she liked him too; she promised to return in a week so that she would not cause him any unhappiness.

She went home, delighted to be with her father. But again, she found herself in the competitive struggle forced by her sisters. Toward the end of the week she dreamed of the palace garden in which the Beast lay dying of sorrow. She felt awful to treat the Beast so cruelly when he had been so kind to her. She even thought, "Why do I not marry him? I am sure I should be more happy with him than my sisters are with their husbands. And I want to do nothing to make him unhappy."

She got up, put on the magic ring which would return her to the palace and found herself back at the castle. She called out to him, "Beast, dear Beast," but there was no answer. Finally she remembered her dream and rushed to the garden; he lay on the ground as though he were dead. Forgetting his ugliness, she threw herself upon him; his heart was still beating so she fetched some water, sprinkled him with it and wept.

The Beast opened his eyes. "You almost forgot your promise, Beauty," he said. "I was determined to die since I could not live without you. I have starved myself, but I shall die content since I have seen your face once more."

"No, no, dear Beast," Beauty cried out passionately. "You shall not die, you shall live to be my husband. I thought I felt only friendship for you, but now I know that it is love." At this the palace was transformed into a place of loveliness and the Beast became well and strong again.

As he rose to his feet, he changed from the ugly Beast to a tall, handsome, graceful young prince who thanked her with tender expression. Beauty sobbed, "But where is my poor beast? I only want him, nobody else." And the prince replied, "I am he." He told her about the wicked fairy who condemned him to his beastly form and forbade him to show any wit or sense until a beautiful lady consented to marry him. And since Beauty had judged him neither by looks nor by talent, but by heart alone, he was free once again.

We must see that Beauty's tenderness brings the terrible Beast to fulfillment. We must understand as well that her acceptance of his ugly animal nature brings her beyond this too-good-to-be-true, virginal readiness to sacrifice her own longings. By coming to love the primitive, untamed being of the Beast, Beauty came to terms with the powerful instinctual forces within herself. The result was that she emerged as a flesh-and-blood woman with a handsome, virile beast-man. No longer was she Daddy's little girl; Beauty was about to lose her virginity.

The Beast of the story is an archetypal motif, a metaphor for the disowned dark side of our heroine, a side which seems ominous and is to be feared, but only so long as its true nature remains hidden in the darkness of the not-me, the land of the shadow.

The shadow is the negative side of the personality, not necessarily a bad or undesirable side. It consists of the aspects of the self which do not fit within the idealized self-image which we each develop in order to make human imperfection more comfortable. Jung himself remains somewhat mired in the moralistic morass which is the residue of the provincial, minsterial childhood background trap against which he rebelled, and from which, in many important ways, he successfully escaped. As a result, his moralistic emphasis undervalues some of the positive value of the shadow. But Jung does make the negative face of the shadow powerfully vivid, and indeed has the inspirational courage to urge each man to come to terms with the personality's potent underside from which he would flee.

> Unfortunately there is no doubt that each person, as a whole, is less good than he imagines or wants to be. Everyone carries a shadow, and the less it is embodied in the individual's conscious life, the blacker and the denser it is.[3]
>
> There is something terrifying about the fact that man has also a shadow-side to his nature which is not just made up of small weaknesses and blemishes, but possesses a positively demoniacal impetus ... a delirious monster ... the blood lust of the beast. ... Out of a dim presentiment of the possibilities lurking in the dark side of human nature, we refuse to recognize it. We struggle blindly against the healing dogma of original sin. ...[4]
>
> In other words, it is quite within the bounds of possibility for a man to recognize the relative evil of his nature, but it is a rare and shattering experience for him to gaze into the face of absolute evil.[5]

Jung instructs us well about the evil of which we are capable. But I find him even more helpful when he emerges from the Victorian perspective which so often limited Freud. In such moments of illumination, Jung helps me stay in touch with the knowledge that nothing that is human should be foreign to me, that the issue is not just one of accepting evil as well as good, but rather one of more modestly and lovingly coming to terms with *what is,* regardless of how it fits with any given conventional morality. It is this aspect that he illuminates when he points out:

> If the repressed tendencies—the shadow, as I call them—were decidedly evil, there would be no problem whatever. But the shadow is merely somewhat inferior, primitive, unadapted, and awkward; not wholly bad. It contains inferior, childish, or primitive qualities which would in a way vitalize and embellish human existence. . . .[6]

One woman's struggle against the delightful aspects of her shadow is transparent in a series of dreams which highlight the inner journey during her pilgrimage through psychotherapy:

> I dreamed I was in the courtyard of a resort hotel, wearing a long, slinky skirt split up the front so that my legs were exposed. A friend of my father's was there; he watched me appreciatively. I recalled how I despised him. He was better educated than my father, and more assertive; and though they both held similar jobs as engineers for the State of Alabama, the other man was always upstaging my father. Though they liked each other to some extent, my father also disliked the man intensely, something he told me but no one else.
>
> As I stood in the courtyard, I moved about seductively, feeling very confident that he wanted me. We went inside his hotel room and I took a bath. I didn't have my own toilet articles, so I used the soap, sponge, bath oil, and towels that belonged to his woman. The items were a lovely shade of pink; I enjoyed them for that reason. I also enjoyed the feeling that her stupid, fat old man wanted me. As I was in the bath, a friend of mine, a woman with whom I had been involved in a close sexual and emotional relationship, came into the room. We laughed together about my seducing the man, and had an extra big laugh about "even using her things!" Then a young man came into the room. I got out of the bath and walked over to him. He held me close to him very

tenderly, and I felt very gentle and loving toward him. I don't know who the young man was, though it feels as though he was a young man in one of my therapy groups toward whom I have loving and tender feelings.

Next I dressed and walked from the bathroom into the bedroom. There were a lot of people in the room; they were having a party. I felt very beautiful. Everyone became quiet, and an engagement announcement was made: the engagement of the stupid, fat man and his woman. She was wearing a garish, hot-pink satin dress, her hair was "salt and pepper" gray, and she was fat. I felt contempt for them both. I also felt very superior, beautiful and smugly aware that the man wanted me, not her.

That night—the night of this dream—and several nights afterwards, I dreamed of weddings. I was the bride dressed in white. I dreamed of having a family with several children. The strangest feeling in the dreams was an awareness of a lack of excitement and vitality. I was getting married, I had a family, everything was as it should be—and I felt bored.

This woman struggles against the shadow of her own lusty, sexy-bitch sensuality. It is reflected in the flashy aggressive older man who was her father's friend in life, her father's own slightly-disapproved-of shadow, a companion he needed but with whom he could not fully identify. While still in the process of exploring her shadow-self, this woman temporarily must restore the balance of her idealized self-image with the duller series of virginal, doughty, bridal dreams. Some day she will be whole, owning her shadow and living with all of her lovely self. (My own struggle with *my* shadow has been no different, no less confusing. Yet it has been exciting and ultimately, rewarding.)

The question then arises, should we not fear Evil? A compelling answer is offered by Dietrich Bonhoeffer, a German theologian and Protestant minister, who knew evil firsthand, living as he did in Nazi Germany. He was at first committed to piety and pacifism but began to see that these forms of goodness were an illegitimate escape from the evil he had to confront during the rise of the Hitler regime. He became an active member of the Resistance movement for which he paid dearly, with years in prison, months in concentration camps, and execution by hanging. In his *Letters and Papers from Prison*, he discusses the ways in which Evil depends on Folly as a mediator for its effective impact:

> Folly is a more dangerous enemy to the good than evil. One can protest against evil; it can be unmasked and, if need be, prevented by force. Evil always carries the seeds of its own destruction, as it makes people, at the least, uncomfortable. Against folly we have no defense. Neither protests nor force can touch it; reasoning is no use; facts that contradict personal prejudices can simply be disbelieved—indeed, the fool can counter by criticizing them, and if they are undeniable, they can just be pushed aside as trivial exceptions. So the fool, as distinct from the scoundrel, is completely self-satisifed; in fact, he can easily become dangerous, as it does not take much to make him aggressive. A fool must therefore be treated more cautiously than a scoundrel; we shall never again try to convince a fool by reason, for it is both useless and dangerous.
>
> If we are to deal adequately with folly, we must try to understand its nature. This much is certain, that it is a moral rather than an intellectual defect. There are people who are mentally agile but foolish, and people who are mentally slow but very far from foolish—a discovery that we make to our surprise as a result of particular situations. We thus get the impression that folly is likely to be, not a congenital defect, but one that is acquired in certain circumstances where people *make* fools of themselves or allow others to make fools of them. We notice further that this defect is less common in the unsociable and solitary than in individuals or groups that are inclined or condemned to sociability. It seems, then, that folly is a sociological rather than a psychological problem, and that it is a special form of the operation of historical circumstances on people, a psychological by-product of definite external factors. If we look more closely, we see that any violent display of power, whether political or religious, produces an outburst of folly in a large part of mankind; indeed, this seems actually to be a psychological and sociological law; the power of some needs the folly of the others. It is not that certain human capacities, intellectual capacities for instance, become stunted or destroyed, but rather that the upsurge of power makes such an overwhelming impression that men are deprived of their independent judgment, and—more or less unconsciously—give up trying to assess the new state of affairs for themselves. The fact that the fool is often stubborn must not mislead us into thinking that he is independent. One feels in fact, when talking to him, that one is dealing with, not the man himself, but with slogans, catchwords, and the like, which have taken hold of him. He is under a spell, he is blinded, his very nature is being misused and exploited. Having thus become a passive

instrument, the fool will be capable of any evil and at the same time incapable of seeing that it is evil. Here lies the danger of a diabolical exploitation that can do irreparable damage to human beings.

Basically, I agree with Bonhoeffer's emphasis on folly as the mediator of evil. The sociological problem that he described—the relationship of the folly of the many to the brutal evil of such a monstrous leader as Hitler—I see as well as a psychological problem in the individual's foolish denial of the unconscious evil within himself. And in this psychological realm, as in the sociological interactions which he described, I also agree ". . . that folly can be overcome, not by instruction, but only by an act of liberation. . . ."[8] Often, patients of mine describe what they do as neurotic or irrational, or, "foolish." In such instances a person will say that he hurts those he loves. But, the patient says he acts out of an unconscious need, or on a compulsive basis, or because he had an unhappy childhood. Certainly the patient wants to do the right thing and tries for a long time to overcome this foolishness, these neuroticisms, but to no avail. The individual then seeks the help of a therapist.

To my patient's surprise, I define such acts as evil rather than as neurotic. Further, I suggest *not* overcoming such things but giving in to them, that is, acknowledging them as individual wishes. The patient should try whenever possible to express them, exaggerate them, and enjoy them. The patient, of course, balks at such satanic support.

One way around this resistance is movement into a fantasy trip. I suggest not worrying about the outcome of this act because it will hurt no one—only we will know about it. After all it is only an experiment. If the therapeutic relationship is trusting enough and the patient is not too anxious, we can proceed. I ask the patient to imagine that he is not hurting others in spite of himself: the things he does in this regard are things he wishes to do. Take for instance a man who has extramarital affairs. He says he cannot help them—they are simply an expression of a compulsive sexual need. He regrets these affairs and feels guilty, out of loyalty to his wife. He fears that if she finds out she will be hurt and angry and there will be trouble for him. I reinterpret his guilt feelings as resentment of unwanted obligations (as Fritz Perls called them). Then I suggest he explore in fantasy. I ask him to describe his affairs as if he had unlimited opportunity, and as if they could be as pleasurable as he dared hope. I ask him to do so in a manner that I might find interesting and entertaining. As he proceeds, he often finds the main complaint is not having as many affairs or as torrid affairs as he would like. His fantasy wishes far exceed his actual transgressions. Putting him in touch with a deep sense of pleasure in having his way helps him own his impulses for such sexual indulgences.

Only then can we proceed with the other aspect of it, that is, the ways in which he hurts his wife. We go into this second phase of evil by my encouraging him to tell me in detail, and in an exaggerated way (so that I don't get any misconceptions) all the things his wife does that hurt *him*. If he can understand how hurt and angry he feels toward his wife, how trapped he sometimes feels in his marriage, how sexually limited he feels by his commitment to marriage itself, his own hurt and angry feelings will emerge with great intensity.

In response, I tend to center on his experience of powerlessness, his feeling that his wife gets her way and that he doesn't get his. At that point, I quickly shift back into his pleasurable extramarital affairs—with emphasis on the fact that she doesn't get her own way then, does she?

Or, that is certainly one time when he gets *his* own way. This tends to elicit a mischievous, sardonic, often satanic smile or laughter. We laugh together in nasty glee, and at this point, he is most likely to get in touch with the fact that his extramarital affairs hurt his wife (or could hurt his wife if she knew about them) because that is *exactly* what he is up to. He cannot get *his* way with her and so he ends up at least in fantasy seeing to it that she does not get *her* way.

The question here involves an examination of his "disloyalty to his wife," as opposed to whether or not he is being *loyal to himself*. No matter how these problems are explored in the therapy session, the patient can no longer define them as neurotic symptoms (that is, as folly). He can see that he is digging deeply into the expression of his own hidden wishes to be more sexually self-indulgent and to win the willful struggle that he experiences with his wife. He can be an evil bastard if he wishes in his marital battle and as far as I'm concerned he can enjoy it; he need only acknowledge it so that it's clear between us and a greater source of pleasure to himself. However, insightfully observed behavior is different from that same behavior carried out as naive folly. Oftentimes, such behaviors are briefly enjoyed without conflict only to be given up as the patient turns to face more directly his struggle with his wife on a more open exchange of dialogue. Energy is then directed at those things in the relationship which really anger him and which he indeed may be able to change (or if not, may learn to live with without feeling threatened and anxious).

As a younger therapist I could not abide the feeling that there were some patients whom I did not like and did not want to work with, even if I could help them. So, acting out of the folly typical of many therapists I tried to work with such people. I was bewildered by my ineffectual efforts and by the patient's lack of improvement and termination of therapy.

I had not yet realized that I had feelings I was not supposed to have. My work in therapy should have been primarily a source of pleasure to me. I should not have worked with anyone whom I didn't like. Instead I foolishly tried to be good. In retrospect, supported by my work in supervising other therapists, I can see how the good therapist, who would never think of getting rid of his patients, unwittingly would do just that via subtle evil ploys ostensibly aimed at helping the patient. At this point I choose to be bad; I am glad that I am, rather than being foolish and unhappy at finding myself so. I feel supported in this by Jung's observation:

> The dammed-up instinct-forces in civilized man are immensely more destructive, and hence more dangerous, than the instincts of the primitive, who in a modest degree is constantly living with his negative instincts.[9]

In psychotherapy it is clear that the hidden forces within any given patient are dangerous to him *only* when he is unaware of them. Even the darkest matters can shed light once they have been discerned and the patient sees them with unblinking eyes. The difference between the wicked and the righteous is not clear unless man sees, in context, how much evil within him he will face. The Hasidic rabbi of Lublin tells us:

> I love the wicked man who knows he is wicked more than the righteous man who knows he is righteous. But concerning the wicked who consider themselves righteous, it is said: "They do not turn even on the threshold of Hell." For they think they are being sent to Hell to redeem the souls of others.[10]

How can it be, you may wonder, that acknowledgement of evil can lead to good? I am reminded of a powerful example in the culture of the Shtetl. Among the Eastern European Shtetl Jews angry arguments are a vital part of life with other people. And when these people fight fiercely with family, friend or neighbor, they feel free to denounce the other person for every sin in the book which can be brought to mind during the argument, that is, every sin save one.

No matter how angry a man becomes in an argument he must refrain from mentioning the one thing that would bring the flush of serious shame to the cheeks of his adversary. He may curse the other man without inhibition, colorfully telling him, "You should lose all your teeth except one, and that one should ache. . . ." Or, "You should burn like a wick and they should put you out with Benzine."[11] But he is never to drench his adversary's face in blood by mentioning the one thing that would shame him.

And so, no matter how wild the fight may become, you do not hit the man below the belt. If you know that the man has an illegitimate child, or that his brother has broken with the Faith, or that his marriage is unhappy, you will *not* say this to him. By knowing clearly the most evil way in which you could shame the other man, you take on the responsibility of fighting ferociously and still treating him with respect. You should never be so cruel as to strike him in the one place where he is most vulnerable.

Certainly I am at my worst as a therapist when I try to feel that I am better than anyone else. At such times I help my patients torture themselves about feeling they are not good enough, that they are to blame for their unhappiness, that if only they tried they certainly could do better. In contrast, those times when I am most aware of my evilness and my limitations, I feel most accepting of my patients as other struggling human beings.

This is expressed in the ways in which I listen to them. And, it often makes me see and communicate how their unhappiness depends upon their asking more of themselves than human beings should. Every thought and feeling is allowed and no action is beyond imagination if only people will face the consequences of their acts. Conventional morality is a game and ethics must be embedded in situations. That is, each act must be judged in terms of its meaning for a given person at a given time rather than in terms of laws cut into stone tablets. Like Zarathustra I support my patients' explorations into the darkness of their own souls, saying: "They will call you destroyers of morality, but you are only the discoverers of yourselves."[12]

Quite often I find my patients are much too hard on themselves. They come to me with expectations that I will judge them, find them wanting, discipline them, and make them good. Part of this is their own projection. It also has to do with my reputation as being a tough confrontational psychotherapist. Indeed I trust my toughness and at times it is a useful resource in my life and in my work.

I am bad all right, but only as bad and as good as other people. In order to be out of danger and live in peace with myself, it is necessary that I clearly see my shadow, the dark side of myself. Every bit of me is worth something, even the evil part. The dark forces themselves can be sources of strength if I avoid the prideful sin of scrupulosity, the self-sorry importance of making my evil worse than anyone else's. We each must learn to look clearly at our list of sins, to take responsibility for our evil urges, and to be able to laugh at ourselves when we take ourselves too seriously.

There is a Hasidic tale that is most instructive:

During his stay in Mezritch, the Rav of Kolbishov saw an old man come to the Great Maggid and ask him to impose penance on him for his sins. "Go home," said the maggid. "Write all your sins down on a slip of paper and bring it to me." When the man brought him the list, he merely glanced at it. Then he said, "Go home. All is well." But later the Rav observed that Rabbi Baer read the list and laughed at every line. This annoyed him. How could anyone laugh at sins! For years he could not forget the incident, till once he heard someone quote a saying of the Baal Shem: "It is well-known that no one commits a sin unless the spirit of folly possesses him. But what does the sage do if a fool comes to him? He laughs at all this folly, and while he laughs, a breath of gentleness is wafted through the world. What was rigid, thaws, and what was a burden becomes light." The Rav reflected. In his soul he said: "Now I understand the laughter of the Holy Maggid."[13]

PART THREE
RE: ORIENT

CHAPTER EIGHT

Back to One

Over the years, again and again, young therapists have come to me for supervision, complaining:

> I'm stuck. For a while the work was going well, but now we're at an impasse. My patient has reached a plateau. He (or she) is blocking and I can't seem to get over this resistance. I've tried to figure out why my patient is doing that but we're fighting all the way.

At times like these it's difficult for the therapist to understand that "a therapeutic impasse" is simply a time when the therapist tries to make a patient do something that the patient is not ready to do. By focusing on the patient's "progress," the therapist engages in a needless power struggle. Getting hung up on how well or poorly the therapist is doing is distracting and drains creative energy from the Work. The most ready resolution for these deadly problems is getting the therapist to shift the focus onto the therapeutic techniques. The therapist must turn attention away from the patient's behavior, away from concern with self-image, and toward concentration on simply doing impeccable work.

The best model I know for getting unstuck is the release from bondage provided by the discipline of Yoga, "the yoke that frees." Though I no longer meditate regularly, the freeing discipline of Yoga serves me well as a metaphor for getting unstuck and from trying to get my own way in my work as a psychotherapist (as well as in the rest of life).

I remember my own early instruction in the breath-counting of Yoga. To prepare myself, I was to sit comfortably each day for short periods at regular times. My mind would be cleared by focusing all of my attention on the edges of my nostrils; at that place where the breath is exhaled.

My guide told me: "You need only breathe in and out quietly and regularly, concentrating on that point. Each time you exhale, you count to yourself, 'One, . . . two, . . . three, . . .' and so on. When you get to ten, begin again."

That certainly sounded easy enough. But my guide went on to warn me of the demons with which I would struggle: "You'll find that you begin, 'One, . . . two, . . . ' and then the thoughts will come. And so it will be, 'One, . . . two, . . .' and suddenly you'll think, 'This isn't working!' At that point you must go *back to one*. You try it again: 'One, . . . two, . . .' and all at once, 'Now I'm getting it.' *Back to one*. Still other thoughts will arise to distract you. Discomforts and temptations will emerge as distractions ('My legs are getting stiff,' or, 'My ass itches') and temptations ('I wonder what it would be like to go to bed with that woman I met yesterday,' or, 'Someday I'll be truly enlightened'). Each time you need only *go back to one*."

At first I did not see why *I* would have to go back to one. I needed only to overcome those thoughts. As if reading my mind, my guide went on: "You'll be tempted to try to dismiss the thoughts, to simply get rid of them. That won't work. It's just another trap. All that will happen is that you'll get deeper and deeper into your insistence that you can overcome the struggles. The only solution each time is to go *back to one*."

It began to sound *not* so easy. I started out with the notion that I was certain to go through the series up to ten and begin again. I could do series after series. Should I count them? "Not to worry," said my guide. "During the first year of breathing meditation most people do *not* beyond four or five. And then come the thoughts, and again it's always *back to one*."

So it is in the practice of psychotherapy. Again and again the therapist has a willful attachment to how he or she is doing, to how the patient is progressing, to the results, to getting his or her own way. All arise as distractions from the work. In each case the solution is to go *back to one*. But first the therapist must prepare a setting in which the basic work can be done. What's more, he or she must have a clear idea of what is to be done and how to do it, or else there is no "one" to which to go back.

To free oneself from the bondage of attachment to its results, it is necessary to be clear about the Work. When we do not concentrate fully on the basic work, we pay attention instead to the patient's "progress," or to our own ego-bound trip ("Look how well—or badly—I'm doing"). Neither path benefits the patient or the therapist. At the point of impasse, the only thing that helps is to go *back to one.*

But to find your way back, you first must know what "one" is *for you.* Clarity about what you do, about how you run the therapy session is absolutely necessary. It is sometimes useful, creative, and fun to vary from the basic parameters of your work. But first you must know the personal baseline from which you are varying. Otherwise how can you know when to return home and how to find your way back?

The therapist, in learning to go *back to one,* returns to fundamentals of the Work; the therapist takes charge of the therapy and leaves the patient in charge of his or her own life. Out of this comes the best work; that *alliance in the absence of blame* in which healing can occur. It is only then that the therapist can offer the expert services of a professional guide. Hence, the impasse born of presuming that the therapist knows what is best for the patient is avoided. By concentrating on the therapeutic work the therapist gets unstuck, leaving the patient free to discover what is desired out of life, how to go about getting it, and at what cost. It is the patient who must choose how to live. When the therapist helps the patient become happier, without needing the patient to change, the therapist's own impeccable work is reward enough.

So it is with the practice of Yoga. Each seeker at first practices Yoga as a path toward spiritual liberation. The beginner initially takes Yoga on as a means to an end. The burdensome efforts of self-discipline are later pursued for their own intrinsic rewards by the more advanced Yogi.

Certain aspects of Yoga can serve as effective metaphors for the work of psychotherapy. Many Westerners think of Yoga as nothing more than a peculiar system of breathing exercises accompanied by grotesque physical postures. Classical Yoga practices consist of more than holding your breath and standing on your head; they have little to do with the Americanized popularization of Yoga as a gymnastic cult of physical beauty and prolonged youth.

Some Westerners imagine the practice of Yoga as an Oriental form of magic, a vehicle for attaining occult powers. Not that special powers do not accrue for the Yogi. Rather it is simply that these *Siddhi* are not what they appear to be. The notorious Indian rope trick is a good example of the cheap magic practiced by fakirs who use Yoga powers for exploitive purposes.

Some years ago an account appeared in the *Chicago Tribune*[1] of two Americans who witnessed such a performance while traveling together in Northern India. They both watched as the rope appeared to unwind itself vertically toward the sky. Just as the conjurer's assistant began to climb the rope, one of the Americans, who was an artist, made a rapid sketch of the scene. His companion, who was carrying a camera, photographed what he saw. Later the photographs showed only a crowd gathered around the fakir, with the boy beside him, and the rope at their feet. Nothing had been suspended but the judgment of the audience. Suggestion or induced hallucination? Perhaps. Levitation? Not according to the photographic evidence!

Among the other Siddhi which develop in the practice of Yoga are those phenomena which we in the West categorize as *para*psychological: extrasensory perception, telepathy, psychokinesis, and perhaps even outside-the-body trips. They parallel the altered states of consciousness and also dramatic instant emotional catharses induced in patients by some Western psychotherapists.

The Indian writers who believe that Siddhi exist view them as distractions from the right practice of concentration and meditation. Sri Ramakrishna calls these by-products mere "heaps of rubbish,"[2] their only importance being obstacles to enlightenment and stumbling blocks in the path to liberation.

Before the publication of *Tales of Power*, an anecdote began circulating in Berkeley, California, about Carlos Castaneda's recent visit to Yogi Chen, an elderly Chinese practitioner of esoteric Buddhism (who is something of a local saint). Castaneda, it seems, told Yogi Chen that he currently was being taught how to produce a "double" of himself. Was there anything similar in Chen's traditions? Of course, said Yogi Chen, there were methods for producing up to six emanations of oneself, "But why bother? Then you only have six times as much trouble."[3] Equivalent psychotherapeutic "magic" creates similar distractions in the treatment process.

How are we to understand a path of self-development that considers the acquisition of the power to perform miracles as nothing more than a trivial distraction from spiritual discipline? This is not true of Yoga alone. None of the Indian philosophies and mystic techniques has either Power or "Truth" as its goal. The West may pursue Progress through Knowledge and Power. The East seeks only deliverance from struggle.

Yoga of one sort or another may be found in all Eastern spiritual paths. In each case the goals are the same: raising of consciousness beyond the distinction between the watcher and the watched, and awareness free from desire. The goal is no less than total deliverance from needless struggle through the non-attachment of knowing that *concern with making things happen is meaningless.*

To understand the discreditation of such powers in the context of Yoga begins with the Indian conception of life as a "wheel of sorrows," turning from birth through the suffering of this life to death and rebirth into yet another round of pain. As Buddha proclaimed: "All is anguish, all is ephemeral."

Human misery is due to the *ignorance* that attributes substance to the illusion that is this life, and to that *attachment* which leads us to hold onto the impermanent things of this life.

To whatever extent we focus on getting our own way, on doing in order to achieve results, on holding on to things beyond our control, we are trapped in needless suffering.

Paradoxically, the Indian conception of universal suffering does *not* lead to a pessimistic philosophy founded on despair. Suffering is not a tragedy, it is a cosmic necessity. Yet each person has a chance to become free of it. For each individual, Karma is the crucial pivot.

Karma is the conception that each act has consequences. Circumstances in this life are the consequences of actions in earlier lives. How we live in this life will determine what our next life will hold in store. It is *not* necessary to believe in reincarnation in order to apply this view to our own lives. Even if we have only one life, we create our Karma as we live it.

We gradually can liberate ourselves from needless suffering. For example, it is possible to effect my future Karma by doing the Work on my Self of raising my consciousness beyond the ignorance of attachment to the results of my efforts. I only get to keep that which I am prepared to give up. In Western terms, Virtue is its own reward. There is no hope of redemption in doing Good in order to be saved. Only by doing Good for its own sake, without seeking reward, can I attain Salvation.

For the patient, psychotherapy may be seen as an attempt to improve Karma in this life. The therapist helps the patient to heighten awareness of the consequences of actions and of the price of willful attachment to getting one's way. In part the therapist plays the role of the guru who shows the patient ways to unhook old patterns by liberation of the self from attachment to the neurotic past.

The therapist offers the enabling practices of treatment techniques, and also the model of non-attachment to the results of these therapeutic efforts as well. The practices and the non-attachment are *both* crucial to the process. Baba Ram Dass describes the Karma Yoga of such offerings by saying:

> ... *the only thing you have to offer another human being, ever, is your*

own state of being ... everything, whether you're cooking food or doing therapy or being a student or being a lover, *you are only doing, you're only manifesting how evolved a consciousness you are.* That's what you're doing with another human being. That's the only dance there is! ... Consciousness ... means freedom from attachment ... You realize that the only thing you have to do for another human being is to keep yourself really straight, and then do whatever it is you do.[4]

There are two primary divisions of these practices, Raja Yoga, the royal path of cultivating the mind and the personality, and Hatha Yoga, the mastery of breathing and other physiological functions aimed at liberating through purification and mastery over the body.[5] In attempting to develop a metaphor for the non-attached practice of psychotherapy, I have focused almost exclusively on Raja Yoga, the Yoga of the will (and particularly on the practices of meditation), and on Karma Yoga, the way of action and loving work.

Meditation begins with *concentration.* At first this sounds simple enough. All that you have to do is fix your attention on a single point. It might be on the tip of the nose, on a thought or action, on a holy saying, or on an image of God. This simple exercise is enlightening in its unexpected difficulty.

> ... it's like trying to take an elephant that has been wild in the jungle and putting one of those iron bands around its leg and then sticking a post in the ground to tame it. When the elephant (like your wandering mind) realizes that you are trying to tame it, it gets wilder than it ever was at its wildest in the jungle. ... It pulls and it pulls and it can hurt its leg. It would break its leg, it starts to bleed, it does all kinds of things before it finally gives in and becomes tame. And this roughly is the tradition of meditation.[6]

It is *not* possible to pursue the meditational path of liberation without straying. Concentration in the practice of Yoga, psychotherapy, or any other spiritual folk art is a matter of developing the ability to *do one thing at a time.* In the practice of meditation, straying from this goal has been characterized as "itching, twitching, and bitching." Most psychotherapy lacks the physical demands of Yoga; it is interpersonal. Therefore, the distractions with which therapists must struggle are focused more on needless evaluative comparisons between how the therapist is doing and how he or she should be doing, or on the reciprocal point of how the patient is progressing and how the therapist thinks the patient should be progressing.

Nonetheless, the problems are fundamentally the same. It is easy for the practitioner of Yoga or psychotherapy to think of other things, to become distracted with remembrances of times past and of other places. Or concentration may be lost by straying into future concerns about how this is all going to turn out. Again, the required correction is *back to one.*

Even seemingly present-oriented self-consciousness serves as a distraction if there is any element of comparison embedded within it. Comparisons are always deadly, whether they pivot around how a person is different or the same as another, or merely around how a person is more different now than before or in the future. The *Law of the Good Moment*[7] holds for the practices of both meditation and psychotherapy. In either case the danger of distracting oneself from concentration in the moment is best expressed by the self-competitive thought, "Here I am, wasn't I!"

The goal is to concentrate your entire being on what you are doing at the moment. Saint Anthony said it well:

> The prayer of the monk is not perfect until he no longer
> realizes himself or the fact that he is praying.[8]

So, when the therapist does the best work, it is not in trying to change the patient, or even in performing psychotherapy. The therapist *becomes* the Work. The therapist *is* the psychotherapy and it all just seems to flow. The irony is that when the work goes this well, it is difficult to recapture in retrospect just what was done correctly.

A parable of Sri Ramakrishna demonstrates that first we must learn to concentrate and only then may we gain a sense of what it feels like to perform impeccable work:

A disciple once came to a teacher to learn to meditate on God. The teacher gave him instructions, but the disciple soon returned and said that he could not carry them out; every time he tried to meditate, he found himself thinking about his pet buffalo. "Well then," said the teacher, "you meditate on that buffalo you're so fond of." The disciple shut himself up in a room and began to concentrate on the buffalo. After some days, the teacher knocked at his door and the disciple answered: "Sir, I am sorry I can't come out to greet you. This door is too small. My horns will be in the way." Then the teacher smiled and said: "Splendid! You have become identified with the object of your concentration. Now fix that concentration upon God and you will easily succeed."[9]

For most of us one lifetime does not seem long enough to attain a state of perfect concentration. In our work as psychotherapists, as in our personal lives, we get distracted, make mistakes, and lose our way again and again. We must learn to give ourselves permission to blunder, to fail, and to make fools of ourselves every day for the rest of our lives. We do so in any case. Scolding and self-recrimination are no more than further errors. Instead we can turn toward the unconditional self-acceptance of one of India's greatest discoveries: consciousness as a witness. To do this you must simply try to

treat yourself as if you were a much-loved child that an adult was trying to keep walking on a narrow sidewalk. The child is full of energy and keeps running off to the fields on each side to pick flowers, feel the grass, climb a tree. Each time you are aware of the child leaving the path, you say in effect, "Oh, that's how children are. Okay, honey, back to the sidewalk," and bring yourself gently but firmly and alertly back to *just looking*. ... "Oh, that's where I am now; *back to work*."[10]

Le Shan's "back to work" is my "back to one." His "just looking" is a reminder that if we are to tame the wild elephant of the mind, we must not beat it.

We recognize that at first it is not easy to get used to staying in one spot. Wild resistance by struggling to be somewhere else is painful and self-destructive.

But willfully trying to force the elephant—or the mind or the patient—to stay calmly in a place where they are not yet ready to stay is also an exercise in futility and needless suffering. Instead we must learn to witness the discomforting interruption and the tendency to stray, without longing, without coercion, and without blame.

> ... when it comes up—it's like somebody who drops by for tea when you are trying to work on a manuscript. You say, "Hello, it's great to have you. Why don't you go into the kitchen and have tea with my wife (if she's not busy, too), and I'll be along later. I'm working on this manuscript." And then you go back to the manuscript.[11]

Whether it's the manuscript or the meditation the work of psychotherapy or life, at such times you simply go *back to one.*

CHAPTER NINE

Already Where We Need to Be

The differences between the Western Judeo-Christian traditions and their Oriental Hindu-Buddhist counterparts can be partially understood as a contrast between a *straight line* and a *circle*. In the West, the secular ideals of hard work, achievement, and progress fit well within the religious burden of avoiding temptation, living the good life, pursuing the straight and narrow course, and striving to imitate the never-to-be-achieved perfect nature of Christ. The straight line that we must follow if we are to be saved is that awesome distance between the badness of who we are and the goodness that is Jesus.

In the circular way of the Orient, we need only recognize that *each of us is already the Buddha;* we need only surrender to our true nature. The guiding principle of the Western cosmos is the higher intelligence called the *Logos,* toward whose perfection we may ascend along that straight line. In the East, the Sanskrit word *Lila* is used in place of Logos. Lila is the term for the Lord's cosmic playfulness through which He creates the illusion of the world by casting all of us (and indeed all that is) in varying modes of His Divine Energy. All that separates anyone from the bliss of *Nirvana* is the *maya* of illusion. Our true nature is at the center of the circle of ourselves (called *Atman,* the Universal Self). As we find ways to give up the struggle to change our ways, we may let go of our passionate attachments to the bondage of trying to be what we are not.

What is often taken to be the fatalism and pessimism of the

Orient is a sense that life is a wheel of sorrows, a continuing cycle of birth, suffering, and death into which people are again reborn through the ignorance of thinking they can change their true natures. Each person's karma is that life into which he is born (sometimes defined as the rewards and punishments inherited from previous incarnations). The karma of this life is the effect of previously led lives and the cause of what is to be endured or enjoyed in future lives.

I do *not* believe in reincarnation. I believe we are not punished *for* our sins, but *by* them. Yet the metaphor of karma is compelling and enlightening. I feel that we are born and we develop into who and what we are largely beyond the power of our will. We may explain our development psychoanalytically in terms of early family experiences, but even so, the issues of personal unhappiness can be attributed to little more than having been born into the wrong house. Had I grown up in the house next door, perhaps I would have been more fully loved, more tenderly accepted, and better appreciated. Who knows?

In life, family and culture encourage us to "improve" ourselves, to develop "good character." Too often the distinction between *character* and *personality* is really the *doctrine of the mask*. At best it covers the differences between the ways other people conceive of our personalities and the ways we know them to be. At worst, the defensive armor of the mask goes even deeper, obscuring the differences between our own noble idealized conceptions of ourselves and the angel-beast of the double soul we truly are at heart.

I believe that biological inheritance and later arbitrary circumstance provide opportunities for joy and necessities for suffering. But just how happy or unhappy I am to be with my personality and my life is largely a matter of how well I accept my fate rather than one in which I demand a reshuffling of the cards, a new deal, or a better hand. I may not always win, but I must continue to play. After all, it's the only game in town. Fighting fate, trying to will that which cannot be willed, or wanting to be someone else living some other sort of life, is an absurd demand to get my own way. This can only invite needless suffering. It's quite enough to experience the suffering that is absolutely required without whining away what pleasures I do have with cries of, "Why me? Why did this have to happen to me?"

Character-building is the denial of the true nature of the self, a search for an improved model. I no longer hope to achieve good character, so long as that implies that my Buddhahood is not already at hand. My aim is not to improve my Self but only to know it more clearly and to learn to celebrate all that I am. I need no more change my personality by building my character, than change my fate by trying to be so good that someone will save me. Remember how many times you said, "Please God, if only this one time You will let me get a passing grade (or a sought-after promotion, or a longed-for sweetheart), then I promise that from now on I'll never lie again (or masturbate, or talk back to my parents)."

This distinction between character and personality is akin to the distinction between *fate* and *destiny*. If I am not willing to know what I feel, to say what I mean, and to do what I say, then my life is that of a passive object of fate. However, to the extent that I am willing to fully accept, to own, to treasure that fortune (or misfortune) which is my own personality, which is myself, then am I able to turn my fate into my destiny. Only then can I become who I am by surrendering willingly to my life as it is given to me instead of trying to be someone or something else.

In order to transform my fate into my destiny, I must give up the romantic habit of telling a bit more than the truth. I must be willing to present myself, as I am, to myself, and then when it is safe, to others. There is no need to hide my strength, my virtue, my special beauty. Yet all of these must be presented in the context of the ordinariness of my weaknesses, my wrinkles, and my warts. William Butler Yeats counsels us well when he tells that "soul must become its own betrayer, its own deliverer, the one activity, the mirror turn lamp."[1]

A life without pain is not possible. Often patients come to therapy hoping that if they can improve their personalities sufficiently, if they can achieve "maturity" or "mental health" then they can live a problem-free life. It takes a long while to learn that:

> In all the world
> There is no way whatever.
> The stag cries even
> In the most remote mountains.[2]

They need not try to become other people, for their hopeless seeking of the ouroboric peace and perfection of reunion with the Great Mother will never be. There is no peace till death, and perhaps not even then. And, ironically, whatever peace there might be comes from accepting the good/bad nature of who we are, as well as the lucky/unlucky quality of our lives.

It matters less that one man is an extrovert engaging in the outer world, while another is an introvert who finds more meaning within himself. It is more important that each be happy with who he is rather than try to be the other. For after all, long before Christ (or Jung), Lao Tzu told us:

> A man with outward courage dares to die,
> A man with inward courage dares to live;
> But either of these men
> Has a better and a worse side than the other.[3]

Perhaps neurosis is no more than the struggle to get our own way, to change others, to correct fate, or failing that, refusing to give in to our own deepest wishes and sense of self, so that if we cannot get *our* own way at least we can keep someone else from getting *his* own way.

I am reminded of a patient with whom I have worked for a number of years who has gotten well beyond much of her depression, is far more expressive, assertive, and creative, and has (in conjunction with her husband's therapy) improved greatly her once unhappy marriage. But she finds it difficult to conclude her work in therapy because of one seemingly insoluble problem.

At first she described the problem as her marriage not being solid or satisfying enough to dissuade her husband from being interested in pornography. Only gradually did she come to see that the problem was really not *his* behavior but *her response* to it. (When he reveals his interest in pornographic books and movies, she reacts with anxiety and resentment as though he were betraying her.)

With my help, she was able to relate these reactions to her distress as a teenager when her father deserted the family and his own unhappy marriage and gave himself over to an affair with a young serving girl. At that time the patient protected herself from the panic of recognizing her total helplessness over these losses by rejecting her father's attentions. As she connected the two events the patient's response shifted from diffuse anxiety and resentment to a bitter, stubborn insistence that she certainly was *not* willing to give in. In other words, she would not accept what she could get from either her husband or her father by tolerating her losses and her dissatisfactions, whatever they might be.

I returned her somber tale with the old Hungarian scissors story. It is told that in Hungary some years ago there was a couple who met, fell in love, and married. At first they seemed very happy until a seemingly trivial argument arose. They cooperated in the wrapping of a package and when it was done there was a bit of extra string to be cut off. The husband said, "I'll get a knife and get rid of the bit of string." But the wife insisted that when she was growing up and packages were to be wrapped, the final bit of string was always cut off not with a knife, but with a scissors. And so the argument began. And for years their marriage was plagued by discomfort and irritability as they argued chronically again and again the dilemma of the knife and the scissors. After a while, of course, the issues were so clear that they challenged one another only by the husband saying, "Knife!" and the wife answering angrily, "Scissors!"

Finally the husband felt he could stand it no longer. He decided that such a stubborn wife must be gotten rid of. Deviously, he invited her down to the lake for a boat ride one sunny summer afternoon. He rowed her out to the middle of the lake, which was quite wide and deep, and there he said to her, "We're going to settle this once and for all. You must either surrender to me and admit that the knife is the proper instrument for cutting the bit of string or I will take this oar and knock you into the water, and since you cannot swim you will surely drown." Her answer was a defiant, "Scissors!" With that, the husband took an oar and lustily swung it, knocking his wife from the boat. Indeed she could *not* swim and floundered helplessly for a moment as her husband demanded, "Knife?" She sputtered, "Scissors," in response, and down she went for the first time. Moments later she fought her way to the surface again. Once more her husband demanded, "Knife?" Spitting water from mouth and nostrils she gurgled, "Scissors!" She went under for the second time. Then, after a bit, exhausted and bedraggled, she reached the surface once more and was about to go down for the third and last time. He said, "Okay, this is my last offer, it's a matter of life or death. Knife, I tell you!" And as she sunk beneath the surface of the waves all that could be seen was her raised right hand, index and middle finger separating and coming together in the mimed gesture of a pair of scissors.

This tale helped the patient laugh at herself as she recognized her own stubbornly spiteful, self-destructive insistence on not giving in. But, she could not shake free of her problem. I offered the analogy of my own struggle with the pain and imminent death which I face daily by my inoperable brain tumor. "What am I to do then?" I asked her. "It is the only life that has been given me. Should I waste it insisting that this cannot happen to me? That it's not fair, that it's too upsetting, that I cannot enjoy the rest of my life because there are parts to it that I find unacceptable? My only hope lies in finding the calm of self-surrender. If I surrender to that which I cannot change, do what I can without attachment to the results, then I will have what I might." Her love for me helped bridge our common human dilemma and she could experience both the absurdity and the profundity of each of our situations. But before she was able finally to be free, she had to journey—in fantasy —into the experience of forgiving her father (and her husband): she had to stop trying to change what she could not change and stop living in the grief over her helplessness. It is enough that we all must suffer losses, disappointments, and betrayals. We need not add to the unhappiness and misfortune which life puts upon us by struggling against our karma, that which is our lot in this our one and only life.

And if the therapist is to help another to find the way, to accept the karma, what manner of man must he be? Again, Lao Tzu is instructive in saying:

> One who knows his lot to be the lot of all other men
> Is the safe man to guide them . . .[4] (for) . . .
> A good man, before he can help a bad man,
> Finds in himself the matter with the bad man.[5]

It is the same for the therapist as it is for the patient. If an individual is to live fully the person must look unblinkingly at all that emerges from his unconscious. If the individual is to be more than a cardboard figure he must peer into the shadow. All that his conscience tells him that he is *not,* secretly he *is.* The aspirations of his idealized social philosophy are no more than denials of the dark underside of what it is to be truly human. A person cannot flee from evil without unwittingly yielding to it. Evil must not be avoided but rather transformed. Should a person try to be generous without acknowledging his own self-interest he will surely turn out to be a prideful despot, giving only when it suits his aspiration to appear benevolent. If charity were anonymous, God pity the poor. Our only hope lies in turning the life of consciousness toward those dark aspects of ourselves which we are taught we should not even think about.

Yet even when we seek to know that which is unconscious in our hidden selves, it can turn out to be merely another form of seeking an unobtainable perfection of the self. Though each person must make a commitment to plumb the depths of his own dark soul, no individual can know it all. The exploration can never be completed; it is the very nature of the beast to be ever partly hidden.

By now, should you feel committed to this exploration of the darkness of the heart, you may be tempted to feel that surely if you try hard enough and long enough, all will be known. The inevitable human pursuit of the illusion of control, of having it in hand once and for all, of no longer having to face helplessness and the loneliness of the solitary pilgrimage through the disturbingly powerful morass of the forces of darkness, will surely tempt you for the rest of your days.

It is instructive to see the limits of the light of consciousness and of the powers of reason in their encounter with the forces of darkness. A story is told of William James, a psychologist who sought to discover and understand all of the varieties of religious experience, and of the success of his failure. In his travels, Dr. James encountered an Indian sage from whom he hoped to get some final answers. Possessing more knowlege than understanding of Oriental philosophy James had learned that it is written that:

> Brahma, the creator, conjured forth eight celestial elephants, which then were assigned to the four corners of the world and the four points between, to stand as support for the upper firmament.[6]

And so he inquired of the Mahatma, "I understand that your people believe that the universe is supported on the backs of great white elephants, right?"

"Indeed, it is so," replied the Mahatma.

"Good, good," Dr. James went on. "Now tell me, just what is it that stands beneath the great white elephants?"

"In each case," the sage replied at once, "there stands another great white elephant."

"And what is beneath that great white elephant?"

"Why, only another great white elephant."

Hurrying on with his inquiry, Dr. James began again, "And beneath that great . . ."

But at this point the Mahatma interrupted. "Dr. James, Dr. James," he responded gently, "before you go any further, I must tell you, it is great white elephants, *all the way down.*"

And so, committed though we must be to peering into the shadows, to facing the dark primordial images, to revealing the rest of ourselves to our consciousness, we must remember that it is great white elephants *all the way down.* Yet we must come to know what we can of what we are, or we suffer the illusions we create by projecting onto others what we cannot accept of ourselves, seeing the enemy as outside of ourselves, living a life of degrading dogmatic defining of others and dehumanizing isolation of ourselves. Because the unconscious provides a compensatory force to one-sided conscious attitudes, the spontaneous self-revelation of our dreams teaches us what we need to know about the parts of ourselves which are usually hidden in the shadows. In this sense, dreams can be prophetic, revealing the triptych of past, present, and future, of where we have come from, where we are along the way, and where we are headed.[7]

Below are written three dreams. They occurred in one night and were presented in one therapy session by a young woman who was several months into treatment. She was experiencing a strange combination of panic at what she was getting into and excitement about where she might be headed.

Dream one: *I am at a cocktail party chatting with some people, I don't know about what. Again and again I see my husband going off into another room with one or another of the women guests at the party. I am surprised to find that instead of feeling jealous, I merely begin to feel curious about what is going on.*

Dream two: *I enter a lavishly decorated powder room. I am appalled to see that the beautifully decorative wallpaper is peeling in many places. I just stand and look at it peeling off the walls without knowing what to do.*

Dream three: *I am in an exciting place. I believe it is a carnival. I am on a platform at the center of things, in charge of some dancing bears. I am having a wonderful time. A man comes by and asks me what I am doing. I am surprised to find that I can answer his question easily. I say to him, "I am the Bear Lady* (she laughs).*" I can see now that that was a pun, meaning I was a lady with no clothes on.*

After exploring the dreams with her at the level of her own personal associations I suggested an overview of the dreams as representing past, present, and future. The first dream represents the past, that is the situation that brought her to therapy. Chatting at the cocktail party represented a superficial, ego-oriented, empty social life. In that dream her husband represented her father on a personal association level and the time he spent with her younger sisters. However, he also represented her *animus*, as characterized by her own husband's actual ventures in a more complex and demanding world than the one in which she lived. By becoming free of her commitment to simple jealousy that is a threat to her ego, this woman has become curious enough to wonder what it would be like to get out of that cocktail-party life and off into another room. And so it was, in part, that she decided to come to therapy.

The second dream represents her present ambivalence and dilemma as she finds that after several months of therapy she is beginning to uncover the shadow side of herself, what she refers to as the "primitive" things in her. At a later session, she admitted that she had not been standing in this dream, but sitting on the toilet, her metaphor for unearthing unconscious material. This is distressing for a woman raised in a family with upper-class standards, with people who feel they are above the experience of ordinary people. Thus it is that she euphemistically refers to the shit house in which she finds herself as a "powder room." She would deny that she functions as everyone else but as Montaigne tells us, "Kings and philosophers defecate, and ladies too."[8] And so despite the lavish decoration of her powder room she finds that the wallpaper peeling away reveals the underlying structure. Her commitment to therapy, to look and see what lies beneath, is experienced now as a kind of helplessness as her *persona* peels away and she is more and more fearful of what she might find beneath it.

The third dream represents her hopefulness and her excitement about the future. The atmosphere is a carnival, when all things are allowable. The dancing bears are her delight and enjoyment of her own instinctual drives, once the dangerously aggressive aspect of them is under control. She knows who she is and she knows what she is doing, and so she can easily answer the question, "Who are you?" asked by her animus. She is the Bear Lady. She has resolved her negative mother complex by taking over the mother aspect of herself. She is the instinctual lady, the powerful woman. And too, she is the *bare* lady. This makes her laugh with delight, that she is the naked, transparent, openly sensual creature who can be what she is for all to see.

My patient's dreams led me to explore further my own wolf dream. Now I could interpret the wolf as my own predatory destructive nature; I live this out as a therapist by committing myself to its other face. That aspect of the wolf is the Romulus-and-Remus Mother-of-Outcasts, nurturer of those faced with destruction. I must yet become the nursed waif who can learn to live with the tamed brutality as well.

Further help came, this time from an old friend who read a journal account of my wolf dream.[9] (You don't always get what you want, but you get what you need.) He sent me a reprint of one of his articles[10] in which he described the work of a German psychiatrist named Levner who developed a technique known as Guided Affective Imagery. My friend's article stressed use of this technique around the theme of feeding-the-beast. For example, the patient is asked to imagine standing on the outskirts of a forest. The patient is told that if he looks carefully a beast will emerge from amidst the trees. As the animal reveals itself in fantasy, the patient experiences negative feelings such as fear, rage, or disgust. But, the patient is encouraged to fantasize approaching, petting, and feeding the animal. If the patient is willing, a transformation occurs in which the dangerous adversary becomes an ally or a playmate. My friend goes on to explain:

> The feeding technique invokes imaginary behavior of a nurturant, supportive, and kindly sort in the face of fearful feelings that have been aroused by a sense of threat. To the extent that the threat and fear are projected and are not appropriate to the situation, the cooperative patient stands a good chance of overcoming them and of freeing himself from their influence over his behavior.[11]

Hence, my patient's third dream and my friend's paper helped me to reclaim my own dark brother. My characteristic counterphobic overcoming of anxiety lead me more easily (both as therapist and as patient) to favor changing places with the beast, to see what it's like to become the dangerous spider when I am trapped in the terror of being the fly caught in the spider's web.

I have cautioned that in seeking to accept ourselves, we must first pay attention to that which is hidden. It is obvious enough that to some extent we hide our *unsocialized attitudes* behind our *persona*. This mask of the social self tells more about the cultural demands that shape our interactions than about those disruptive instinctual impulses which culture seeks to tame. And psychoanalysis has for many years made us aware of the need to understand the *repressed contents of the personal unconscious,* which underlie the more rational, reality-oriented aspects of the *ego*. Jung has added to our understanding of what is hidden through his concept of the *shadow,* that disowned or not-yet-revealed aspect of the self which includes not only the personal unconscious but also the *archetypal motifs of collective unconscious* and the *inferior functions of a particular individual's psychological type*.

Out of my own struggle, I emphasize recognition of the freedom to be powerful in a tough world. But you are right to be wary in following any of my advice because "for men with different types of psychological makeup, different types of ethics are appropriate."[12] Even so, hear what I have to say, let it be your option if you want it, but set it aside if you do not. What I wish to tell you is that it is crucial that we not fool ourselves.

When we can, we must act lovingly. But when anger, aggression or even violence is called for we must learn to strike out expediently, effectively, and with gusto. I try to act honestly, openly and with compassion and tenderness toward those I love and even toward others who pass my way with whom I have little stake but who merely do their own thing without jeopardizing my well-being. However, in the presence of my enemies I must be able to fight like an alley cat. Margaret Mead once said that manners are useful in dealing with people with whom we don't get along. Honesty is for dealing with friends; I save diplomacy and aggression for my enemies.

All of this would seem clearly destructive and cynical if people were indeed simply good or at least respectable. But as Machiavelli points out, as men are not good, it is sometimes necessary to invoke the force of a lion or the cunning of a fox. If that fine Italian hand is too cynically manipulative for your humanistic sensibilities, then look instead to the great and ancient subcontinent of India, that traditional seat of reverence and peace. Modern Western humanists have looked to the Orient in recent years for a model of spiritual freedom, inner peace, and nonviolent means of attaining social accord. But this idealized social model has an often unexamined underside. "The blank pessimism of the Indian philosophy of politics (is) untouched . . . by any hope or ideal of progress and improvement."[13] And so it is that in the *Mahabharata*, a traditional Indian work of practical guidance, four chief means of approach to an enemy are outlined. They include *Saman*, the way of conciliation or negotiation; *Danda*, the rod of punishment or retaliatory aggression; *Dana*, or bribery; and *Bheta*, or splitting and sowing dissension as a means of dividing and conquering. And finally, ironically, *Maya* is added to these four chief means of meeting an enemy. Maya is usually defined as the illusory nature of everyday life which must be seen through, transformed, and given up in order for an individual to reach the level of spiritual awakening and freedom. But, in this context Maya is defined as a trick, a deceit or the display of an illusion with which one might snare an enemy. Other minor devices are suggested, such as *Upeksa* (which means overlooking, or pretending not to be concerned because one is not ready to make a decision about involvement in any particular affair) and *Indrajala* meaning the net of the god Indra—India's Zeus—which involves all the varieties of stratagem and tricks of war). These suggestions constitute "the seven ways to approach a neighbor in this unsentimental ocean of the fish,"[14] under the doctrine of *Matsya-nyaya,* the Law of the Fishes: *The big ones eat the little ones.*

We must not mistake manners for morals. Life can be merciless and pain a necessity. John Steinbeck somewhere once pointed out that we need only look in a tidal pool to see life in the raw: there we may observe the predatory Law of the Fishes in action. The big ones who eat the little ones is part of *man's* animal nature as well. We may build temples, offer charity for our fellow man, make paintings and play music, but *first* we must survive! And at times that means one of us is going to get hurt; it's going to be either you or me and if it's up to me, I promise that it will be you.

So, what is hidden must be revealed before what appears to be can assume its true shape and substance. Yet I would caution against the *psychoanalytic fallacy* that only what is hidden is really true. A man who acts and speaks lovingly of his woman may reveal in a fantasy, in a dream or through a slip of the tongue some underlying hitherto unconscious hatred of that same woman. This certainly does not mean that he *really* hates her. It need only suggest that in addition to that one-sided positive feeling, there is a shadow, an ambiguity, a basic human polarity. *Impurity is the only reliable criterion for the reality of any feeling.* For me, this man's love would be more believable if I saw it in the face of the hatred which must accompany it. If truly "pure," it would seem too good to be true. So far as I know, I have never in my life had a pure motive.

This need to accept the other side, the shadow side, is one of the bases for the Trickster-Healer's *Be Where They Ain't* approach. One patient's response to my shadow-revealing trickery was to experience her struggle with me (really with the underside of herself) as "Fighting the Windmill." She described it this way:

> I know I'm better because I feel worse.
> The nicer you are, the harder it gets.
> The stronger I grow, the weaker I feel.
> You can't give it to me because I already have it.
> I can't be littler because you're not bigger (damn it!).
> The more lost I become, the clearer it gets.
> I'm feeling confused, I must be in the right place.
> I move the furthest when I'm stuck.
> The worst part is knowing that I can make it.
> The safest places are the most dangerous.
> The more I cry, the harder I laugh.
> The more I try, the harder you laugh.
> The more I love, the more I hate.
> The more I fight, the more friends I have.
> I can't make you love me, you already do.
> I can't be special, everyone/no one is.
> Given permission to rest, I work harder.
> When I rest you call it work; When I play you call it
> work; When I work you call it work. I can't mess
> up (damn it!).
> Since I can't please or displease you, guess I'll just have to do what I
> want.
> I don't get to win, but I don't have to lose.
> There is no winning or losing, but I get to keep what I have.[15]

It is not possible to appreciate the light without knowing the darkness, the heavens without the earth, the dry lands without the sea, warmth in the absence of cold. *Human* lacks meaning if *animal* is unknown, just as being a man takes its shape most fully in the presence of woman. Angel and devil are Janus faces. Cain cannot be understood without knowing his brother, Abel, and much of Jesus is incomplete without Judas.

The transformation brought about by the recognition and acceptance of the hidden shadow-identity does not turn the person into someone else so much as it completes him. So it is that I would amend the traditional Hindu Story of the King's Son:

There was a king's son, once upon a time, who, having been born under an unlucky star, was removed from the capital while still a babe, and reared by a primitive tribesman, a mountaineer, outside the pale of the Brahman civilization (i.e., as an outcast, uneducated, ritually unclean). He therefore lived for many years under the false notion: "I am a mountaineer." In due time, however, the old king died. And since there was nobody eligible to assume the throne, a certain minister of state, ascertaining that the boy had been cast away into the wilderness some years before was still alive, went out, searched the wilderness, traced the youth, and, having found him, instructed him: "Thou are not a mountaineer; thou art the King's Son." Immediately, the youth abandoned the notion that he was an outcast and took to himself his royal nature. He said to himself: "I am a king."[16]

I believe that nothing changed in the sphere of facts, only his awareness was transformed. Was he a Prince who believed he was a mountaineer, or a mountaineer who at that moment realized he was also the King's son? Perhaps it was only that, "he is united, at last, with the hidden fullness of his own true nature."[17]

I do not argue for an Oriental reconciliation by the ultimate harmony of opposites so much as for the need to recognize and cherish the existence of the other side. My goal is not some idealized perennial peace and absence of conflict, but rather a vital and viable state of dynamic tension. I seek not agreement but rather a balance of forces, both of which are needed. Politically, for example, I know that when the Left is victorious, the liberators soon become the new oppressors who must be acted against so that the fluid flow of human process can go on. My commitment is to the ebb and flow, the rhythmic ever-changing, never-changing state of flux, of life on the move.

Having emphasized at some length the need for making things more vivid by exposing what is hidden, I would like to turn now to how we are to *become what we are* once all of it has surfaced. The fullness of my vision will once again be brought forth by turning my gaze Eastward, this time toward the twenty-five-century-old Hindu singing of *The Song of God: Bhagavad-Gita.*[18]

The Bhagavad-Gita is a powerfully poetic battlefield dialogue which takes place before an epic encounter of a long-ago civil war among royal Indian kinsmen. It is a dialogue between one of the commanders, Arjuna, and Sri Krishna, an incarnation of the Supreme Godhead who takes it upon Himself to appear in the form of Arjuna's charioteer. A family power struggle has arisen among the offspring of the sons of King Vichitravirya. The King's eldest son was born blind, and so his younger son, Pandu, took the throne when their father died. The elder brother raised his sons bitterly and with stubborn determination that someday they should reclaim his lost seat of power. And so these young men have come to challenge Pandu's sons in battle. The sons of Pandu, Arjuna and his brothers had been willing to work out a sharing of the power, but their bitter and dispossessed cousins force a battlefield confrontation instead.

Our Lord Krishna has offered to mediate between the warring cousins but only in accordance with the wishes of the antagonists. He offers the forces of His army to either of the opposing sides, and to the other, Krishna Himself as counsel and advisor. So it was that He became the driver of Arjuna's chariot. On the eve of battle, Krishna drives the chariot into the open space between the two armies so that Arjuna may view the enemy hordes. Recognizing so many of his kinsmen, Arjuna is appalled at what he must do and exclaims in despair: "I will not fight!"

Krishna instructs Arjuna on his alternatives and helps him see what he must do. Though the commander is enlightened by his charioteer to the effect that he *must* fight, Krishna's teachings are by no means warlike. (To appreciate what He has to offer us even today, we must understand the battlefield as a metaphor for one aspect of life, and Arjuna's caste as a symbol of his identity.) At that time in India men found themselves divided into four categories:

Seer and leader,
Provider and server.[19]

These categories reflect the four Hindu castes: the *Brahmins* who were priests, the *Kshatryas* who were warrior-politicians like Arjuna, the *Vaishyas* who were merchants, and the *Sudras* who constituted the servant class.

Krishna tells Arjuna that there is more than one solution to his problem just as there are many paths to fulfillment, alternate ways to find release from spiritual bondage, and more than one way to seek enlightenment. Yoga is the term for such personal Oriental disciplines, for the ways in which one may seek release from the trap of life's endless sorrows. Krishna describes to him the Yoga of Renunciation (the ascetic way), the Yoga of Meditation (the inner seeking), the Yoga of Mysticism (through faithful surrender to the Divine), and the Yoga of Devotion (through worshipful love). But is it toward *Karma Yoga* that Krishna turns His disciple, and toward which I turn your attention.

Karma Yoga is the doctrine of salvation *in* the world, in life *as it is,* by *becoming who you are.* It is not possible, of course, *not* to act, *not* to live your life, *not* to be yourself. "All are helplessly forced to act."[20] But the way to salvation is to act by giving yourself over fully to the moment by *renouncing the fruits of your activity.* All activities must be performed, not in terms of what you seek to be or how well you hope to do, but in accordance with who you are and what you feel here and now.

In the Bhagavad-Gita, the nature of your particular life is defined in terms of your *dharma,* or duty, which you find in the *karma* of the life into which you are born; the karma of the personality is the *you* of your one and only life. And so it is that Krishna instructs Arjuna:

> Do your duty, always; but without attachment. That is how a man reaches the ultimate Truth; by working without anxiety about the results.[21]

You need only discover who you are, and act according to the tendencies of your own nature. The most important aspect of your life and your personality is simply that it is *yours* and no one else's. As Kirshna tell us:

> It is better to do your own duty, however imperfectly, than to assume the duties of another person, however successfully. Prefer to die doing your own duty; the duty of another will bring you into great spiritual danger.[22]

Better your own life, imperfectly performed, than the life of another, well performed. In every life, in each particular human being, *Brahman,* the Holy Power, is present and each person can perform his or her own particular Act of Truth:

> The story is told, for example, of a time when the righteous king Asoka, greatest of the great North Indian dynasty of the Mauryas, "stood in the city of Pataliputra, surrounded by city folk and country folk, by his ministers and his army and his counselors, with the Ganges flowing by, filled up by freshets, level with the banks, full to the brim, five hundred leagues in length, a league in breadth. Beholding the river, he said to his ministers, 'Is there anyone who can make this mighty Ganges flow back upstream?' To which the ministers replied, 'That is a hard matter, your Majesty.'
>
> "Now there stood on that very river bank an old courtesan named Bindumati, and when she heard the king's question she said, 'As for me, I am a courtesan in the city of Pataliputra, I live by my beauty; my means of sustenance is the lowest. Let the king but behold my Act of Truth.' And she performed an Act of Truth. The instant she performed her Act of Truth that mighty Ganges flowed back upstream with a roar, in the sight of all that mighty throng.
>
> "When the king heard the roar caused by the movement of the whirlpools and the waves of the mighty Ganges, he was astonished, and filled with wonder and amazement. Said he to his ministers, 'How comes it that this mighty Ganges is flowing back upstream?' 'Your Majesty, the courtesan Bindumati heard your words, and performed an Act of Truth. It is because of her Act of Truth that the mighty Ganges is flowing backwards.'
>
> "His heart palpitating with excitement, the king himself went posthaste and asked the courtesan, 'Is it true, as they say, that you, by an Act of Truth, have made this river Ganges flow back upstream?' Said the courtesan, 'By the Power of Truth, your Majesty, have I caused this mighty Ganges to flow back upstream.'
>
> "Said the king, 'You possess the Power of Truth! You, a thief, a

cheat, corrupt, cleft in twain, vicious, a wicked old sinner who have broken the bounds of morality and live on the plunder of fools!' 'It is true, your Majesty; I am what you say. But even I, wicked woman that I am, possess an Act of Truth by means of which, should I so desire, I could turn the world of men and the worlds of the gods upside down.' Said the king, 'But what is this Act of Truth? Pray enlighten me.'

" 'Your Majesty, whosoever gives me money, be he a Ksatrya or a Brahman or a Vaisya or a Sudra or of any other caste whatsoever, I treat them all exactly alike. If he be a Ksatrya, I make no distinction in his favor. If he be a Sudra, I despise him not. Free alike from fawning and contempt, I serve the owner of the money. This, your Majesty, is the Act of Truth by which I caused the mighty Ganges to flow back upstream.' "[23]

We make a mistake if we ask ourselves, "Am I good enough?" or, "Is it worthwhile to be me?" Whoever or whatever we are or do is who and what we are supposed to be. It is our Act of Truth. Psychologically, many of our problems began when, as children, someone led us to question the worth of our particular existence or performance. Whoever heard of a baby who was inadequate or a child who did not know just exactly how to be a child? How could it *not* be all right for me to be me? How could it *not* be just right for you to be you? The Divine Spark of every single person is just that he is that particular person, whether we define being human in the Western Judeo-Christian tradition of the Messiah:

How should a messiah behave? Now tell me. Do you know? You know only one thing: that he relieves your pain, your precise pain. He is messiah to your particularity.[24] ... A particular man saves ... (one other) particular man;[25]

or whether we define humanity in the Oriental Hindu-Buddhist tradition of the universality of the Supreme Being who Himself says:

Whatsoever is the seed of all creatures, that am I. There is no creature, whether moving or unmoving, that can exist without Me. I am the gambling of the fraudulent, I am the power of the powerful. I am victory; I am ethic. I am the purity of the pure.[26]

It is the joker of the Tarot deck, The Fool, who is wise enough to ask, "Who am I?" Innocently and openly, he steps forward into the unknown so that he may become who he is. Upright, he makes the right choice. Reversed, he will mistake his identity and live some other's life.

Our only hope is to learn to yield to each moment as it is and in the best way we can, to live life as a work done as much as possible without anxiety about results "in the calm of self-surrender."[27] Only then can we fully live our own lives and be ourselves by engaging in just what we are doing at the moment, by doing it our way, by being able to declare *not* that our life is perfect, but that imperfect as it is, surely it is *ours alone* and nobody else's. For Krishna tells us:

> When a man acts according to the law of his nature, he cannot be sinning. Therefore, no one should give up his natural work, even though he does it imperfectly. For all action is involved in imperfection, like fire in smoke.[28]

And in response, we can then rejoice in the surrender of becoming who we are, as does Arjuna when he answers:

> By your grace, O Lord, my delusions have been dispelled. My mind stands firm. Its doubts are ended. I will do your bidding.
> ... OM. Peace. Peace. Peace.[29]

PART FOUR

AWESOME IMAGES

CHAPTER TEN

The Great Mother

I guess you could say that my main problem with women is my stubbornness. Although I know better, I somehow never fully give up the fantasy that someday I will get to understand what a woman is all about. Understand, I'm not your run-of-the-mill Male Chauvinist Pig. My wife, Marjorie, has taught me much about what it might be like to be a woman. And she, who knows me well enough, is the one who declares that I am the most liberated man she knows with regard to the issue of women's rights, that is, a man who views women as fully equivalent human beings. Yet she also points out (at the damnedest moments) that at those times when I do *not* seem enlightened, I am as lunatic as other men in my misunderstanding of what the hell women are all about.

When I am wise enough I look to women to instruct me about such matters. And so they do, but part of what they teach is that some of what I might learn is beyond my comprehension. Such discouraging messages come from not only the obviously militant advocates of female politics like the Woman's Liberation Movement leaders, the Lesbian Gay Liberation spokeswomen, and female writers such as Simone de Beauvoir and Sylvia Plath; a simpler, less sophisticated, non-political, anonymous Abyssinian woman offers the following absolutely devastating description of her feminine experience:

> How can a man know what a woman's life is? A woman's life is quite different from a man's. God has ordered it so. A man is the same from the time of his circumcision to the time of his withering. He is the same before he has sought out a woman for the first time, and afterwards. But

the day a woman enjoys her first love cuts her in two. She becomes another woman on that day. The man is the same after his first love as he was before. The woman is from the day of her first love another. That continues all through life. The man spends a night by a woman and goes away. His life and body are always the same. The woman conceives. As a mother she is another person than the woman without child. She carries the fruit of the night nine months long in her body. Something grows. Something grows into her life that never again departs from it. She is a mother. She is and remains a mother even though her child dies, though all her children die. For at one time she carried the child under her heart. And it does not go out of her heart ever again. Not even when it is dead. All this the man does not know; he knows nothing.[1]

How then can I begin to understand that creature who both completes and confounds my world, that being who is so much like me and yet is a significantly wholly other as well? Frankly, one of my inclinations is simply to try to *use* women to fill my own needs without struggling with the heavy responsibility of keeping in mind that they are human beings with their own sacred souls. I'd like to say that I don't give way to this very often *because* I am deeply respectful of the separate humanity of the women in my life space. But the truth is that I don't try to use women because when I do, I am most open to being used myself. Maintaining the illusion that I am in control is futile, lonely, and in the long run always more costly than the effort is worth.

I remember early in my practice treating men who "used" prostitutes. All they had to do to control these women was to give them some money and they could manipulate them into doing whatever they wanted. They could make a whore not only do any sexual trick they commanded, but could get her to be nice to them as well. If such men couldn't buy love, at least they could rent it. The women needed the money. The men had it. The women had to give in. The men were contemptuous, superior, in control.

Later in my practice, I began to treat some hookers and strippers. They made it clear to me that the Johns with whom they dealt were suckers. Give them a little sexual excitement and you could get them to pay all the money they had. Men were so easy to control.[2]

The degrading easy exploitation of prostitution is the most obvious form that men and women have of using each other as objects. But, the subtler and more deadly things we do to each other are far more common. In the microcosm of European Jewish Shtetl culture,[3] the men spend much of their time studying the Talmud, exploring the Law of the Holy, while the women administer matters of hearth and home. There is much political exchange of appearing to respect the importance of each other's role, but beneath the veneer of such courtesies is deeply felt contempt.

The men really believe that the women are too ignorant, foolish, and shallow to appreciate the sacred writings of the Torah. Let them be the servants to man that God intended them to be; let them cook and clean without thinking or feeling. The women, beneath their public deference to men, see themselves as running the real world while the men nitpick in the world of religion and ideas like small boys at play. But the loss of a mate whom one can respect and trust is only part of the sacrifice: the loss of part of the self is even more costly.

I remember well a very beautiful young woman, a call girl whom I began to treat several years ago. She wasn't a $10-a-trick street-corner hooker; she was Class-A Capitol Hill—a $100-a-night companion and lover. But aside from the social setting, the emotional dynamics were the same: a hooker is a hooker. She came to me because she was depressed. She had the same emptiness and sense of futility that all hookers carry inside. She was a willful, seemingly self-indulgent, emotionally-detached human being who used sex as decoration, as an instrument for profit, as a weapon to degrade men (without recognizing that at each point she degraded herself as well).

Over a period of months the work went well and she moved, as she wanted to, from a career as a prostitute to the next level of such work in our culture: she became a cocktail waitress, still trading seduction for cash, still manipulating, still keeping her heart out of it. She would show up at my office during a break in her work, dressed to the nines; usually she wore a low-cut, elegant, but a bit too obvious, floor-length velvet gown. It would be split up one side almost to her hip exposing a long, lovely, mesh-stockinged leg and high-heeled silver shoes. In her hair was an overdone rhinestone tiara to set off her rococo makeup and costume jewelry. But when she entered the office she'd drop into a leather chair like a little girl and say, "This is the only comfortable chair in this whole lousy town. Can I take my shoes off?" And she'd settle in, and we'd talk of what her life had been like and how it was now. And often she'd cry.

She worked hard. As things started to work out she got herself a boyfriend. He wasn't a customer, but someone she truly liked. Of course, in the process of transition she unfortunately chose someone who had problems of his own. And so she involved herself with an older, married man who eventually "betrayed" her by going back to his wife. She was hurt and furious. She'd let herself be vulnerable and for the first time she was the one who was hurt.

She left the office that day swearing revenge; somehow she was going to get him. She returned later in the week for our next appointment. She was absolutely furious with me! She told me that I'd ruined everything, that once she had been able to take care of herself and now she no longer could.

What happened was that she lured her lover back to her apartment one last time. She wanted to make him feel as helpless as he made her feel. She described the scene: she got him into bed, determined to excite him, to raise him to a fever pitch; then she would throw him out. She turned him on in ways that she had learned in a thousand other beds. She was getting things just where she wanted them, and then—she turned to me and said, "It's you, you bastard, you with your therapy. You ruined everything. Just when I had him where I wanted him, *I got excited!*"

It seems as though the only way any of us can "use" someone else is by temporarily giving up a part of ourselves. So be it! My trying, as a man, to deal with women by using them as objects will get me nowhere worth going. What then are my other options? I'm tempted to go back to where it all began, to the first woman in my life, to my mother. In my struggle to make my way through this complex male/female world, it has in fact been helpful to examine my early mother/child experiences, to sort out the remnants of that personal history, to disengage the impact of its unfinished business from the present reality of my adult relationship to women who are my contemporaries. But there are maternal forces at work in my life that are not the product of that long-ago struggle with my now deceased, sometimes missed, good/bad biological Bronx mother. There are as well the primordial, dark images which churn out of the Unconscious. These I share with all other men: the archetypal images of the Great Mother.

In Tarot, one aspect of the Great Mother appears in the Star card. This naked maiden, pouring the waters of life, inspires hope, and promises that great love will be given and received. The forebodings of doubt and pessimism expressed when the card is dealt upside down threaten loss of love.

In times of great distress, moments of overwhelming fear or pain or weariness, I long for the refuge that a good mother could provide. Though some of us would rather not face that tender hunger deep within us, at such moments the mother-longing inside each of us rises. For some it echoes a lovely safe time when as babies the good mother was there to provide all of the needed care and nourishment, comfort, warmth, safety, and protection that was desired. But many of us never had that lovely maternal care, never felt at one with a mothering provider of union, pleasure, and peace. And still we long for such a surcease of pain and anxiety with a powerful nostalgia, as though searching for some state once achieved and now lost.

How can it be then, that a man can long to recapture something that never really existed in his own personal history? How can he miss that which he never had? The personal mother whom each of us experienced always figures with monumental significance in the shaping of our lives. Not only does she affect us directly in terms of the ways in which her personality and behavior influenced the vulnerable, half-formed children we once were, but she also functions as the accidental carrier of the powerful archetypal experience of the Great Mother image.

No mother, whether loving or cruel, no matter how dependable or inconsistent, will be experienced by her child solely in terms of her actual performance, or only in terms of what really went on between them. Each mother will be burdened with the child's ambivalent reactions to the opposing archetypal aspects of the Great Mother, she who is both loving and terrible.

Each child imbues his own personal historical mother with the multiple images of the Great Mother Archetype.[4] The kaleidoscopic imagery which elaborates the pale figure of the "real" biological mother (she who raised you) intensifies the experience of each child and haunts the imagination of each adult.

For many of us the fundamental importance of the Great Mother has been obscured. We who have been raised in the Judeo-Christian tradition of Western culture assume a myth of creation which begins with the preeminence of the Great Father who made all that is—who created man. In Genesis we find the traditional patriarchal version of a paternally founded humanity, with woman created as a playmate/companion and servant of man.

However, there are other earlier creation myths in which we can recognize the Great Mother as the source of all things. The patriarchal reduction and distortion of her status is reflected in the diminished remnants of her epic which remain in the tale of Eve and the Serpent. So it is that in the earlier Accadian Creation Epic, we are told:

In the beginning the world was without form and void. And our Great Mother Eurynome rose naked from the abyss, and, looking about her, found that she was alone. She danced in the darkness, and by her dancing the air was set in motion. Wind blew upon her face from the north, and she took it in her hands to rub it, giving it the similitude of a speckled serpent.

This same serpent lusted after our Mother and she suffered him to cast his coils about her body, and to know her. But as yet he had no name.

And in the process of time our Mother took the form of a dove and brooded upon the face of the water and was delivered of a great egg; which the Serpent coiled about to hatch it, so that it split open and all things were created.[5]

In all primitive myths, it is the female rather than the male who gives life.

The longing for the union with the womb-containment of the Good Mother to which I have referred is merely one aspect of the recurrent complex themes of the maternal archetype. But it is the first one, and therefore a fitting aspect with which to begin. Rejoining the Great Mother often is expressed in spiritual longings for mystical experiences in which the individual regains his place as an undifferentiated part of the cosmos. To be at one with the Universe, as in oceanic experiences, is to know union with the Great Mother at the time of Beginning without End. Perfection, wholeness, unmarred satisfaction, complete contentment describe such a paradisiacal reunion. All is Unconscious, total dependence, unexamined bliss. We are all haunted by such longings. In each of us is the Taoist seeking to be the fish that loses itself in the water.

You cannot defeat the Great Mother! So long as your adult life is defined against the biological mother of your childhood, you are confusing her limited importance with the overwhelming power of the dark haunting images of your psyche's active imagination, with the deep-felt shadows of the collective unconscious. These are feelings we all share, regardless of the quality of our upbringing.

At some point in therapy, once the patient has examined present attitudes in light of unfinished childhood longing, I sometimes turn attention to the individual's helplessness before the Great Mother. As the patient struggles to finalize the relation to his childhood, I may simply insist: "Like it or not, *Mother won*, and *you lost!*" This confrontation with helplessness often seems intolerable to the patient, who is further dismayed to see that even the ways in which he chooses to fight this helplessness (whether by submission or by rebellion) have been defined by Mother. What is he to make of this defeat by the all-powerful mother when he has already come to see that Mother is just another human being who herself was raised by her own good/bad mother?

Only increased courageous awareness can help. The patient must face the awful ambiguities of adulthood if he is to be free. To move away from the hope of ever being reunited with the Great Mother means solving your own problems every day for the rest of your life. It's such a heavy responsibility; it doesn't seem fair at all. It's wearying and none of us ever will be completely free of the temptation to try to go back. But facing this awareness is the only way to escape the siren song of the womb/sea of the Unconscious, the haunting call to return to the Great Mother. To make his way, man must follow the hero's journey. He must move toward awareness by heeding the call to adventure, accepting the aid of magical helpers, eschewing those who would tempt him to give in. He must endure his ordeals, slay the dragon, journey to the underworld and finally return with his newfound wisdom.[6]

A woman's struggle with separation from the Great Mother (and with the men who would defeat her efforts) is analogous; but in significant ways it differs from a man's struggle. Erich Neumann's analysis of the myth of *Amor and Psyche* throws clear light on women's struggle for freedom.[7]

Psyche, like her fairy-tale counterpart, Snow White, is a mortal maid of such unspoiled beauty that she is loved by everyone and adored by every man who meets her. People inevitably compare her with the goddess Venus (Aphrodite) and find the maiden more desirable. Venus, the mythic representation of the Great Mother archetype, is goddess of beauty and all else that is female. And, like Snow White's "Mirror-mirror-on-the-wall, who-is-the-fairest-of-them-all?" stepmother queen, she is intensely vain, jealous, and possessive of the men about her. When she becomes aware of how mortal Psyche is worshipped, Venus cries out in rage:

Behold, I the first parent of created things, the primal source of all the elements; behold I Venus, the kindly mother of all the world, must share my majesty and honor with a mortal maid. . . . But this girl, whoever she be, that has usurped my honors shall have no joy thereof. I will make her repent of her beauty. . . .[8]

Venus appoints her son, Amor (Eros), to be the instrument of her vengeance. She instructs him to make Psyche tragically fall in love with the vilest of men. Psyche learns of her projected fate when an oracle prophesizes her death in marriage to a monster. By surrendering to her fate, Psyche finds that she can claim new options and ends up living a luxurious life married to an invisible husband who comes to her only in bed and in the darkness of the night.

Her anonymous mate is, of course, Amor, who is too taken with Psyche's charms to kill her, as his mother had commanded. Yet his perception of marriage is the unenlightened mating that includes abduction and rape. Caught in the primitive instinctual surrender to the male, which was the lot of the unliberated female, Psyche " . . . unwittingly, yet of her own doing . . . fell in love with Love."[9]

Psyche's envious sisters appear on the scene and urge her to disregard Amor's insistence that he be invisible to her. They tell her she must discover what he looks like lest she be mated to a monster. These sisters represent Psyche's own shadow-side, her wish to be free of male domination. Guided by them, she brings an oil lamp to the darkened bedside of sleeping Amor and discovers that he is no monster. Once she dares defy him by bringing the light of her own awakening awareness to their relationship, she recognizes him as a god, one whom she views simply as a beautiful man. This beginning of higher feminine consciousness required the support of her sisters, just as it does in today's consciousness-raising groups. By taking a more active role, Psyche celebrates her own individuality and serves as an archetypal model for women's emergence.

But in seeking awareness of just who Amor is (as well as clarity about whom she herself has become), Psyche inadvertently burns him with a drop of scalding oil from the lamp of her newfound consciousness, at the same time accidentally cutting herself on an arrow from his quiver.

> Psyche's act leads, then, to all the pain of individuation, in which a personality experiences itself in relation to a partner as something other, that is, as not only connected with the partner. Psyche wounds herself and wounds ... (her husband), and through their related wounds their original, unconscious bond is dissolved. But it is this twofold wounding that first gives rise to love....[10]

Hurt and angry, Amor goes home to the Great Mother, Venus. Psyche seeks to reclaim her lover and evokes further wrath from Venus. To redeem herself, Psyche must take on heroic labors which Venus sets for her. (It is not enough for a woman to free herself from male domination, she must go on to reclaim her femininity in new and difficult ways. She must accomplish great things on her own, with courage and independence, but in a way which redeems the best of female power without simply acting like a man.) And so she does, staying in touch with the unconscious instincts as she calls upon her earth powers to accomplish labors as terrible as a journey to the underworld.

Sent on her way by the Great Mother, Psyche defeats evil by accepting it in herself (unlike the male hero who must slay the dragon). By bringing together opposing goddesses who represent separate aspects of the maternal archetype, Psyche reunites the Good Mother with the Bad Mother, reclaims the unity of her own female power, and regains her lover in a transformingly new love relationship. By asserting her own independence she reveals Amor's mortal aspect, attains her own divine aspect from the Great Mother, and gives birth to a human divine child who reflects the delicate yet powerful interplay of the eternal ambiguity of the man/woman relationship.

The whole damned male/female relationship remains both delightfully and exasperatingly ambiguous to me. Militant female liberationists argue that there are no *real* differences of ability and approach between males and females. They contend that role and attitudinal differences are learned (and consequently can be unlearned), that the seeming sexual differences have been encouraged solely as a means for men to continue to exploit women, and that anyone who says differently is a Male Chauvinist Pig.

Because I believe completely in the need for women's rights to be supported fully, this seems like a hell of a time for me to insist that there may well be inevitable, inherent sexual differences. Yet, aware of the dangers of being misunderstood (or even of being unwittingly abusive to others), with characteristic male heroics, I will discuss some of the aspects which I believe differentiate men and women; differences which lie at the heart of their value and of their danger to one another.

Recently, there has been a good deal of compelling and worthwhile discussion of female sexuality. Important affirmations and clarifications are available of the equivalence of women's and men's erotic desires, of the role of clitoral orgasm, of the right not to have unwanted babies, of the woman's body as her own (rather than as "belonging to her man"). The redressing of the implied sexual inequities are women's due, and ultimately they will be to men's advantage. What then (if anything) will remain of the differences which may continue to contribute to heterosexual fulfillment? I continue to believe that men and women are not simply biological variations of the species, with mere trivial differences limited only to their sexual and reproductive functions. Males and females seem to me to have reciprocities of attitude and ways of being which complement and complete one another in the most creative ways, though these differences may at times be their greatest sources of conflict. So, I see sexuality as a metaphor for creativity.

Here again Jungian archetypes can be helpful, particularly his concepts of the *Anima* and the *Animus*. Jung suggests that in the transpersonal unconscious of every man is his Anima— the woman in him—just as within every woman there lurks her Animus—the unknown aspect of her that is male. Men and women not only share a common humanity, but perhaps even their differences potentially are not insolubly alien each to the other. It is only that some modes are more readily available to the male while others to the female. Perhaps it is only to the extent that I can accept the woman within myself that I can ever hope to understand women, to receive all that they have to teach and to offer me.

Yin and Yang are the ancient Chinese vital principles of the universe, the fundamental polar categories which maintain life's state of tension when in opposition and effect its harmony when together. Yin is the Feminine Principle and Yang is the Male. The ancient Taoist sage, Lao Tzu, in describing to Confucius his voyage to the World Beginning, tells:

> The mind is darkened by what it learns there and cannot understand; the lips are folded, and cannot speak. But I will try to embody for you some semblance of what I saw. I saw yin, the female energy, in its motionless grandeur; I saw yang, the male energy, rampant in its fiery vigor. The motionless grandeur came about the earth; the fiery vigor burst out from heaven. The two penetrated one another, were inextricably blended and from their union the things of the world were born.[11]

Originally neither yin nor yang was more important than the other. At first they merely referred to one side or the other, like of a hill or of a river. Gradually they began to acquire reciprocal characteristics such as darkness and light, so that one had no meaning except in contrast to the other. Yang, the male principle, came to be characterized as sunlike from heaven: bright, firm, creative. Yin, the female principle, represented the earth, the moon: dark, yielding, sustaining.

At first these modes were equivalent primal powers, both completely necessary aspects of existence. Some radical feminists would argue that life begins as female and that the earliest and best developed civilized culture was a now-lost matriarchal society which modern man only mimics and distorts with his oppressive patriarchy.[12] There is some evidence that the concepts of yin and yang may have suffered some comparable distortion.

The earliest known Chinese culture in which they appear is the Shang Dynasty, which consisted of hunters who developed to the pastoral stage; they were shamanistically led believers in a world filled with spirits. But more significant in this context, the Shangs were a totemistic matriarchy who believed "the female was the animal of change, the animal that could bring about transformation."[13] However, the female power of the mare gave way to the male power of the dragon when, in the twelfth century B.C., a neolithic Western tribe called Chou invaded the area and replaced the Shangs as the dominant power. Perhaps, as is often the case, the godlike figures (or in this case the goddesses) of the pantheon of the conquered people are relegated to lesser and more demonic positions in the conquerors' spiritual hierarchy. By the time of the Chou Dynasty, yin began to take on aspects of negativeness, weakness, and evil in contrast to yang's newfound positiveness, strength, and inherent goodness.

So far I have suggested only a few of the fundamental characteristics of yin and yang. There are far richer images described in the *I Ching*, the 3000-year-old Chinese *Book of Changes*. It is a volume filled with fundamental folk wisdom. Like the Bible it is an oracle, and also like the Bible it offers better guidance than prophecy.

In the *I Ching*, yin appears as broken lines while yang appears as unbroken ones. They are combined into hexagrams symbolizing the fundamental interplays of the female and the male forces in their mediation of the way of life. The basic male three-line figure is called Ch'in, and the female is called K'un.

Ch'in, the concentration of the yang force, denotes father and:

> ... suggests the idea of heaven, of circle, of a ruler ... of jade, of metal, of cold, of ice, of deep red, of a good horse, of a thin horse, of a piebald horse, and of the fruit of trees. A door open. In Ch'in God struggles.[14]

K'un, in contrast, denotes the mother and:

... suggests the idea of the earth, of cloth, of a cauldron, of parsimony, of a turning lathe, a young heifer, of a large wagon, of what is variegated, of a multitude, and of a handle and support, among soil it denotes what is black. K'un represents compendious receptivity, and response to Ch'in. K'un completes the great beginnings originated by Ch'in. Think of a door ... closed. The greatest service to God is done through him in K'un.[15]

These alternating primal states, yin and yang (the feminine and the masculine principles) expand and contract, grow and diminish, come and go like the night and the day, as "sooner or later everything runs into its opposite."[16] So it is that the cold and the warm seasons give way one to the next. Who is to say one is more important that the other? Unfortunately some men do choose to give preeminence to one over the other. In consulting the Chinese *Book of Changes*, the seeker is urged to remember that:

The New Year commences in February, before the Spring's Equinox and opens the six months of creative activity which come under the domination of the forces of yang. During this time the masculine pursuits of farming, hunting, building, and marrying are all important.

The yang phase passes its peak in June, prior to the summer Solstice and wanes until it is superceded by the forces of yin, which begin their reign just before the Autumn Equinox in September. During the second half of the year more docile, feminine activites come to the fore; weaving, recreation, the planning of the year ahead, childbirth.[17]

Despite such pejorative distortions of the feminine characteristics, it seems to me that there is some basic wisdom in the Taoist doctrines of the yin and the yang. Most important for me is the insistent reminder that there cannot be one without the other, that each has qualities needed by the other, that the masculine and the feminine principles complete one another as they alternate as rhythmically as the tides. Their equivalent significance amidst their significant differences is for me the model for my relation as a man to a woman, and also as one human being to every other human being. Kurt Vonnegut points out that it is a grave error to mistake or let:

... old-fashioned writers ... make people believe that life ... (has) leading characters, minor characters, significant details, insignificant details ... lessons to be learned, tests to be passed, and a beginning, a middle, and an end.[18]

There are differences certainly among human beings, and some clear ones I believe between men and women, but it is in our sexual and our human differences that we are perhaps most alike. The Taoist doctrine of differences and similarities which underlies the interplay of the yin and the yang (and our foolishness about them) is clearly stated in the ancient parable "Three in the Morning":

There was man who kept monkeys. He told the monkeys, one time, that their acorns would be rationed: each monkey would get three acorns in the morning, and four acorns in the evening. The monkeys were infuriated. And so the keeper said, "Look, I am not an unreasonable man. We will change this. Each of you may have four acorns in the morning, and three acorns in the evening." And with this the monkeys were all pleased.[19]

The strong surge of feeling I experienced while writing these last few pages makes me aware that this is my center and perhaps my only real contribution. Whatever specific differences in the sexes I may come up with will certainly be less moving observations to me (and I assume to you, the reader) than is my sense of isolation in this world of people. In the male/female separation, I feel the loneliness, the terror, and the void most clearly. And so only now, in this writing, do I come to understand how much my longing to be a woman—to bring forth the womanliness in myself—is partly my wish to be less alone, to be less firmly imprisoned in my own separate skin.

My experience as a psychotherapist suggests that the most comon match-ups for marriages in our culture are in the direction of the obsessional male to the hysterical female. At best, the obsessional male can be described as logical, thoughtful, realistic, capable of attention to detail and planning ahead, stable, and self-contained. At worst, his wife may complain that he is too reasonable, unresponsive, hardheaded, detached, cold, picky, and unfeeling. The hysterical female, on the other hand, may be described at best as warm, affectionate, emotionally expressive, imaginative, and capable of deep feelings. At worst her husband may complain that she is emotionally demanding, that she greatly exaggerates her complaints, is unstable and undependable, and has no sense of logic whatsoever.

This match-up of seemingly gender-bound characteristics brings about the completions of the male by the female and the female by the male that make for the richest and most fulfilling aspects of marriage. Paradoxically, this intermesh also leads to the most exquisite pain, misunderstanding, and seemingly unresolvable conflict.

As a family therapist, or at least in my work with couples, I have a distinct advantage. My own marriage, you see, can be described much better as the mating of a somewhat obsessional female with a colorfully hysterical male. At my best, then, I have a good deal of the woman-in-myself available to me which makes me much less likely to side disproportionately with the men in the couples. In my own best view of myself I have little need for logic, much commitment to feeling, and a much greater trust in intuitive understanding than in scientific inquiry.

Be that as it may, from whichever side we approach marriage or mating, it behooves us to seek people who will complete our own skewed or self-limiting approach to total humanness. Marriage literally can be viewed as seeking, if not the "better half," at least *the other half.* It becomes a way of finding—in the other—a compensation for our own imbalance. At worst, of course, it's a matter of simply finding someone else to blame. But even that has its place in our difficult trek through the world as single, isolated, and only partially developed individual human beings.

It is tempting to try to find some further understanding of the difference between male and female in the homosexual analog. Of course, the differences we find again may be more the result of centuries of cultural impact than of some fundamental biological diferences between the sexes. Nonetheless, let us take a look and see what we find.

One of the differences between male and female homosexual coupling is that there are among male homosexuals many more brief, faceless encounters—pickups of strangers in public places—which involve fleeting and explicitly sexual interplays, sometimes without one person getting to know the other's name. This is less true of female homosexual encounters. It is my impression as well that male homosexual couples tend to have relationships of briefer duration than lesbian couples. It may well be that males bring less of a sense of relatedness to their homosexual relationship, less instinct for nesting, or continuing supportive nonsexual feelings.

This tends to be supported by my own impressions of the differences between male and female homosexual relationships which are brought about in institutionalized settings, such as reformatories and prisons. In male correctional institutions, the typical relationship is characterized by the dichotomy of the "wolf" and "punk." The wolf is the aggressive, pursuing male homosexual who exploitively intimidates the younger, more passive male homosexual, the punk. He offers protection and rewards for the punk's cooperation, and brutal punishment for his reluctance. Most of the relationships place emphasis on explicit and somewhat impersonal sexual exchanges.

In contrast, the homosexual relationships of institutionalized females are more lasting, social, and elaborate. They tend to congregate into "family" groups with designations such as "aunt," "uncle," "niece," "nephew," "cousin," with much more emphasis on communal living. They tend to get to know each other better, there are more affectionate and social exchanges, and less of the anonymous and exploitive explicitly sexual interchange common to the male homosexual.

All of these observations are in general fitting with the yin/yang distinctions and with popular characterizations of men as strong, active, and aggressive, as opposed to women who are often seen as weak, passive, and submissive. All of this then fits with men being viewed as sexually exploitive while women we are told are more vulnerable because of their need for love as a grounding for sex. These stereotyped descriptions are further supported by a vision of men as logical and fond of detached abstract thinking, instruments of Logos; women on the other hand are understood as being emotional, intuitive, mediators of Eros. Women are thus seen as more in touch with their Unconscious and with the fundamentals of everyday living. They allow Nature to flow through them rather than to fight actively to conquer it as a man is thought to do.

It seems to me that these caricatures and distortions of gender resist clarification and eradication not only because they serve the dominant male in his political oppression of the female, but because they are *not* totally incorrect. Instead they create as much mischief as they do and are as difficult to dispel because they just barely miss the mark. They are grotesquely subtle distortions of actual differences which create confusion and irrelevance. And, they are not so totally made up out of whole cloth as to be transparently wrong enough to be understood and gotten rid of easily.

My only hope is to substitute descriptions of the sexual differences which avoid any suggestion of one being superior to the other. The best recent explorations of these matters which I have come upon are presented by a very wise woman who also happened to follow her career as wife and mother with many creative years as a Jungian psychotherapist. Irene Claremont DeCastillejo, in her touchingly profound book, *Knowing Women*,[20] describes some of the differences between women and men in terms of varying sorts of awareness (thus eschewing the popular characterization of women being less aware). Her own writing is a movingly vivid example of female consciousness at its best as she demonstrates the feminine gift for *relatedness* in her enlightening exploration of "meeting" and of "bridges" in the living terms of immediate experience. She explores memorably the differences between man's "focused consciousness" and woman's "diffuse awareness" by describing the "basic woman" as one in whom:

Everything is accepted, enjoyed or hated as a whole. She feels equally at one with the stars or a drop of dew, a rose or a blade of grass. She does not analyze them nor want to do anything about them. She is simply aware. For man and again I refer to the extreme male, the scent of a rose is not enough. He must learn all he can about it, prune and graft the plant to obtain even better roses. No woman, as woman, does such things. They would not occur to her.

This female *relatedness* is aimed at meeting unique, singular events without concern for formulating general rules about their occurrence. After all, a woman understands that a particular interaction between people happens only once, and that abstract speculations about it deaden its immediacy and cloud the intuitive grasp of its once-and-for-allness. Attention to the feelingful aspirations of the particular human qualities of the people involved makes it irrelevant for the feminine force to try to make up unreal conceptual laws about them. *Masculine* conceptualization thrusts toward *mastery* while *feminine* understanding moves toward *contact*.

I find it difficult, yet absolutely crucial, to remain aware of these differences in approach of the male and the female without deeming one more important than the other, one superior and the other inferior, one the center and the other the surrounding ground. The reciprocal interdependence of the masculine and the feminine, of the yin and the yang is concretized visually in the eternally fucking black-and-white fish which symbolically represents the Tao, the uncarved block which is the natural way of life to which we must submit, the great water of nature in which we fish must lose ourselves.

As a man, I must listen closely to what women have to say if I am to be instructed. Eleanor Bertine (yet another woman therapist of Jungian persuasion) writes of her understanding of the relation of the yin and the yang, of the psychological sense of the roles of the feminine and the masculine principles:

The two together are essential for a complete personality, the masculine giving the forms, the feminine the color. But the principle of one's own sex should always be in the ascendance, with the other presence in a complementing capacity.[21]

Each of us must allow the emergence of the principle of the opposite sex within ourselves. A man must listen for the voice of his anima, of his woman within. And each woman would be wise to harken to her animus, to the concentration of yang force within herself which will offer her own masculine resources and balance when she needs them. Bertine stresses the need, at the same time, to keep one's same sex principle in ascendance. (For myself, and for most men I know, the greater danger of the two appears to be the risk that our feminine natures may be totally excluded.)

It may be that during this time of women's striving for independence there is some greater temporary risk of their masculine upsurge overwhelming the primary feminine identity. I am reminded here of the rhetoric of Jill Johnston, a militant Gay Liberation Feminist who insists:

Until all women are lesbians, there will be no true political revolution.[22]

And indeed the Lesbian Gay Liberationists have been a significantly supportive factor in the Women's Liberation Movement. A comparatively small group of these homosexual women have brought strength and dedication to the Movement unimpeded by dependence on the male. Yet beyond a certain point they seem more a part of the problem than of the solution in this critical aspect of human evolution. Woman must come to her own maleness (as man his femaleness) but we all need to be aware of the demonic force of our shadow as it emerges from our hidden consciousness lest the solution be worse than the problem.

Perhaps it is enough to say that for the moment men are more in danger of completely missing the woman in themselves, while women must take care to resist being overwhelmed by the man in them. At another time in history, the dangers might be reversed. By way of example of the male side of this struggle, I would like to share part of a letter from a good friend whose lifelong struggle with his anima helps him understand my own:

> I still am not able to separate passivity, castration, paralysis, and defeat from the sweet gentleness of acquiescence. In fact, I experience them as having to coexist. At the very same time I know I must resist at all costs giving in, that I must hold perfectly still and not utter a single cry of protest as I am being beaten and tortured, at this self same time, I know there is a gentle, loving, comforting companion who never leaves my side although I cannot always see or hear or feel her.
>
> It has been my impression that ever since the brain tumor was diagnosed, this gentleness has become much more evident in you, has occupied a much larger part of your ego. Naturally, I see the tumor as a material manifestation of the negative, devouring Mother. Therefore, I believe a compensatory element has emerged in consciousness, and it is this aspect in you, as in myself, that I seek to establish contact with.[23]

By pointing to the risks in finding the rest of ourselves, I do not mean to suggest in any way that they are not risks worth taking. A man out of touch with his feminine side, like a woman who has disowned the masculine aspect of herself, is a caricature of what a complete person might be. And if a person is out of touch with the anima or animus aspect of the opposite sex, surely that person will be an enemy to the personification of that disowned opposite sex when he meets it abroad in the person with whom a life will be made.

Again I will let a woman instruct me on the knowledge that I cannot disclaim one aspect of myself without losing some of the valued remainder of my nature. Here is one woman's dream that tells the story. The dream reads:

> I saw a woman sleeping. In her sleep she dreamed Life stood before her and held in each hand a gift—in the one Love, in the other Freedom. And she said to the woman, "Choose!" And the woman waited long; and she said, "Freedom!" And Life said, "Thou has well chosen. If thou hadst said 'Love,' I would have given thee that thou didst ask for; and I would have gone from thee, and returned to thee no more. Now, the day will come when I shall return, and that day I shall bear both gifts in one hand."
>
> I heard the woman laugh in her sleep.[24]

CHAPTER ELEVEN

The Death Card

Of all the forces of darkness, surely death is the darkest. And now I would speak of that dark force of death, of my own death, of the death of loved ones, of enemies, and of yours.

The Tarot image of this darkest of all the archetypes is the mysterious black-armored, skull-faced horseman on the Death card. Everyone is equally powerless before the inevitable onslaught of this dark rider. Upright, this Tarot card promises destruction followed by transformation and renewal. Dealt in the reversed position, bodes only unchanging stagnation.

When my wife and our three sons moved with me to Washington at the beginning of 1961, our lives underwent a pivotal change. During the first three and a half years, my wife's mother died and then my father and then her father and then my mother. It was like a series of hammer blows to the head. At age 35, I suddenly felt like an orphan. Our prolonged grieving, our sense of being alone in the world, and the recognition of our own impending deaths were compounded by my wife's and my own independent decisions to give up contact with the remaining members of each of our own families after the deaths of our parents. Those other relationships turned out to be more emotionally destructive than sustaining.

When my father was dying I was deeply pained but could not stay at his side to the end as I would have wished. He developed acute leukemia and died within three weeks of the onset of obvious symptoms. He was confused by everyone's lies that he was merely suffering from a curable form of anemia. I talked to my mother about telling him the truth, but she felt that was a bad idea. Since he was her husband, I did not feel I had a right to interfere. It was very painful to see his perplexity and confusion. (In the terminal stages there was a blood seepage into his brain resulting in aphasic difficulty in word-finding and subsequent frustrated outbursts of temper.)

In a more lucid moment he called me to his bedside and asked me to explain to my mother that he really did not want to argue with her but that he was having a difficult time getting his words straight. I promised to try to help her understand and I did. Soon after, he was dead.

My father had been generous with everyone but himself. I remember how proud he was at age 58, when he finally bragged to me that he had bought two suits of clothes at one time, more than he absolutely needed. At 58, he had finally bought two suits. At 60, he was dead. I took the few thousand dollars that I eventually received as an inheritance and bought a big new, red air-conditioned Riviera automobile.

Two years later my mother also developed acute leukemia. I remember that a resident at the hospital stopped me in the hall and asked if I was indeed the son of a father who died two years before of acute leukemia and a mother who was dying of the same disease. I said that I was. He said, "You have a very interesting genetic background." He looked frightened and confused when I told him to get away from me before I killed him.

The entire clan of aunts, uncles, and cousins was at the hospital day after day. (One of the things my family does well is conduct a death watch.)

I was pained deeply to see my mother dying, to see her hurting and afraid, to anticipate my own loss. Curiously, I found myself upset that this should be happening at the beginning of the summer, that it might ruin my vacation. It was enormously helpful to me to get beyond my guilt, to forgive myself for so humanly trivial a bit of self-concern.

My mother was having a very difficult time because she felt awful and frightened while everyone told her she was doing just fine. I spoke to the doctor, an old family friend, and he advised strongly against telling my mother that she was dying. The family was outraged that I should even consider it. I decided it was up to me to choose and that with my father gone

I needed only to check with my sister. I asked her what she wanted to do and with usual conviction and support she said, "You decide."

And so I went to my mother's hospital room and did one of the most difficult things I have ever done. She was complaining about how everyone was treating her. I told her that the trouble was that she didn't realize what everyone else knew—that she was dying. I knew that in her own way she tried to live well and now, I told her, there was a chance for her to die well.

I guess she really knew, because all she said was, "Well, maybe I can do it if you just tell me how long I have to go." I told her she had two or three days. We cried a lot and held each other.

Those three days were the best days my mother and I ever spent together. She was straight and strong and beautiful. She called in each person that she loved, told them she knew she was dying, and tried to tell them what they meant to her and how much she would miss them.

At times it was tough for her. The fear and the pain were overwhelming. At one point she asked me to bring her some pills so that she could kill herself. I was torn, but I refused; I asked her to live with her pain a bit longer so that I would not have to live the rest of my life with the pain of knowing that I helped her kill herself. She forgave me, but I don't know that I have yet forgiven myself.

The night she died, the night before the funeral, I dreamed that I had come to visit one of my cousins, the one I like best in my family. I visited her at a private mental hospital which symbolized my familial compound. I came as a relative rather than as a therapist. As we walked around an inner courtyard and talked, she reached over as if to kiss me on the cheek. But instead she tore a piece of my cheek out with her teeth. It was then that I awoke and decided never to see the family again after the funeral. They had some things to offer that I wanted but their destructive prices were too high. It's been almost ten years and I haven't seen any of them since then.

I still miss my mother and my father at times. The death of

loved ones causes a painful aching in the chest, sobbed out in fragments, in bits and in pieces. And just when you are sure that you've gotten it all completely settled, you turn an unexpected corner and run into another chunk of longing.

However, the death of enemies is a far different matter: it is a time for celebration. I still can savor the delight of learning, some years ago, that a man who spat out hateful words all of his life died of cancer of the mouth. He was a destructively bigoted southern senator who projected onto blacks ("niggers" he called them) all of the attributes of himself which made up his own unexamined shadow. His death filled me with pleasure.

Facing my own death is so very different than witnessing anyone else's. At times of pain and weariness, it offers some small promised comfort of relief at last. But I also have spent many weeks crying, grieving my own death as the loss of someone I love. At times I found myself intrigued and frightened by fantasies of life after death, but each time I give them up. Without knowing for sure, I am certain that death simply will be the end of everything that is me. The greatest pain is in having to give up everyone and everything I love.

For a while, beginning with my first operation, I struggled to deny my helplessness by trying to do something about the money so that I could take care of all of my loved ones after I died. I suddenly realized that I had too little insurance and even less in savings. I struggled to rectify things, only to be turned down as a bad risk by one insurance company after another. Finally one company offered to insure me on a high-risk policy, the premiums for which would cost a ridiculous amount of money. Ignoring the fact that I would be working too hard in the time that remained to me, I seriously considered taking the policy. That night I dreamed I was building a pyramid. I woke to realize that I was denying my mortality, and in so doing was throwing away what life I had by constructing a posthumous memorial to my own greatness. Instructed by the dream, I recounted it and told my feelings to my wife and my sons. I informed them that I had decided *not* to take out the policy.

They were beautifully loving in support of the shadowy wisdom of my dreaming self.

Instead I try to face my helplessness and have turned myself toward enjoying life as it has been given to me. I do this by being myself as much as I am able, and by giving myself over to the pleasure of being with people I love and doing things that have meaning for me. I'll take what I can get and make of it what I can.

Many years ago I remember an article on the front page of the *New York Times* which announced the prediction by a number of astronomers that in several million years the earth would come so close to the sun that all life on this planet would be destroyed. The item caught my interest and I discussed it with a number of people. To my amazement, many of the people to whom I related this prophecy reacted with despair, most often expressed by exclamations such as: "Then what the hell is the point of working so hard and trying to plan for the future!" So focused were they on the final outcome that the precious immediacy of each moment of their own particular lives had become obscured.

Sometime ago I began to play the Game of Epitaphs with my patients. Many of them seemed to be looking only toward outcomes in which they lived out their lives in a style set up primarily to prove to others that they were good enough, or to prove to themselves that they could somehow win. Their anxiety about results sullied their enjoyment of the experience of who they were and what that felt like.

As a way of summing up in a terse but tellingly poignant way what they might be missing. I asked them what they would like to have as a final gravestone comment. They then would offer an epitaph and sometimes I would offer an alternative capsule memorial. Some of the epitaphs the patients wrote for themselves were: "She took good care of others," "He never let anyone down," "At least she wasn't a burden," and "He never lost an argument."

At that time several years ago, when this graveyard game

began, I was concerned about recognizing that I myself was sufficient whether or not anyone else approved. Because of that, as my way of doing my job and of showing patients that they had other options (whether or not they chose them), I would often offer my own chosen epitaph: *"He did his best."* Later on, as I learned to be easier on myself (and so on my patients as well), I amended my own final after-death description to: *He did his best ... when he could."* But since my recent immersion in confrontation with the imminence of my own death, even that seemingly self-accepting epitaph feels too rooted in results and effects to be a fitting capstone to my own brief but just right existence. Now, were I to bother to choose an epitaph, it would better be: *"He died as he lived ... his own way."*

In the end, death comes to all men, as it is coming to me and as it will surely come to you, and puts a period at the end of each man's story. But to the extent that any man has become who he is, then he may die as he lived, as his own person. "And death shall have no dominion."[1] Just as with the way to live, the way to die is *your own way.*

Let me speak of one particular man's death by retelling the Hasidic tale of Bontche the Silent One.[2] At the time when Bontche quietly died many years ago in a small village in Poland, no one seemed to notice his passing. Who knew whether this simple, uncomplaining, unassuming man died of a work-weary broken back or a world-weary broken heart?

Quietly he had lived, and quietly he died. All his life he had suffered his misfortunes in silence, gone his way in a barely noticeable manner of peace, humility, and hard work undertaken without complaint. When kindness toward others was a possibility, he gave freely but unobtrusively. When he himself was in need, he accepted help but never demanded it. He was silent in life and silent in death, speaking not a word against God and not a word against men.

And when he died, he was met at the Gates of Heaven by Abraham himself. Welcomed by an assemblage of angels, Bontche could not believe their warmth and admiration were meant for him. They smiled and coaxed him insistently, until in silent bewilderment, he entered the Heavenly Court, fearful that his poor feet might sully or mar the perfect beauty of the gem-studded alabaster floor. It took a great deal of angelic urging and persuasion to convince Bontche that the Lord indeed had taken smiling notice of his silent self. And not only that, but God had issued a Divine Order that Bontche was to dwell in Heaven for all of Eternity and to be given anything and everything that he desired. Convinced at last, Bontche smiled and replied, "Well if that is to be so, could I have maybe a fresh roll and a glass of hot tea?" Hearing his wishes the angels looked down, a little ashamed.

The death of Bontche the Silent One is as touchingly unassuming as was his life, but even the death of a man who has lived cantankerously befits *that* man in his own particularity. That sullenly removed philosopher of history, Georg Hegel, for example, died as he lived, cantankerously:

> ... on the very point of death (surrounded by his disciples) he only raised his head a little. "I had one pupil who understood me," he was heard to mutter; and while everyone present became alert to hear the venerated teacher pronounce the name, his head relaxed again to the pillow. " One pupil," he went on, "who understood—and he misunderstood."[3]

I myself am neither as sullenly removed as Hegel nor as unassuming as Bontche. I am no lofty abstract philosopher, nor could I ever be described as a humbly peaceful silent one. I am deeply involved in intensely intimate relationships, a singer of songs, a teller of tales, and am easily given over to fighting the good fight, caring more for the struggle than the outcome. Like Cyrano, when Death comes, I shall meet him in my own way:

> Let the old fellow come now! He shall find me
> On my feet—sword in hand—
> ... I can see him there—he grins—
> ... that skeleton

—What's that you say? Hopeless?—Why very well!—
But a man does not fight merely to win!
No—no—better to know one fights in vain! . . .
I knew you would overthrow me in the end—
No! I fight on! I fight on! I fight on.[4]

Surely I will be defeated by the Forces of Darkness. I want only to lose in *my own way*, being myself though beyond hope of victory, without concern for the results—only because it is yet a last instance of *becoming who I am*.

PART FIVE

THEATER, THERAPY, AND EVERYDAY LIFE

CHAPTER TWELVE

It's Only Tragedy

Some common experiences seem a fundamental part of every human being's sense of life, but tragedy is *not* one of them. Compare the concept of the *tragic* with the idea of the *holy*.[1] Almost every language has a word for the experiences of "the holy." All over the world we find this concept, not as a designation spread from a common linguistic source by cultural diffusion, but rather as a term arising out of the need of every group of people to describe a universal human experience.

This is not the case with the term "tragic." Tragedy is no more than an early Western form of literature which fits well our particular now-failing cultural legacy; but it remains no more than a literary conceit nonetheless. The term did *not* arise out of humanity's cradle to describe some basic common human phenomenon. It does *not* appear everywhere. It is *not* the way of Everyman.

Tragedy was originally a sixth-century B.C. Greek word, coined in Athens some 2500 years ago to describe a particular kind of play then in vogue in that ancient city-state. No other language has a word for "tragic," except as it has been taken over and adapted from the original Greek theater term. Tragedy, like nationalism, is a costly and burdensome evaluative elaboration, a cultural device, and a historical extravagance rather than a biological necessity. It is an inessential and limiting category of interpretation whose time has passed.[2]

The phenomenon of *theater* itself does appear everywhere, even in the rites of the earliest primitive communities. Shamans and worshippers, dressed in animal skins, chant and dance as they portray rituals of the births, deaths, and resurrections of gods and spirits. True enough, the modern conception of theater in the history of western civilization begins in first great theatrical age of sixth-century B.C. Athens.[3] It is there that the three elements of theater first emerged: actors who sing or speak independent of the original unison chorus; dialogue which conveys an element of conflict; and an audience whose participation in the action is limited to its emotional involvement.

It was in this age of the glory of Greece that actors first performed in place of priests, in hallowed areas set aside for those performances, yet these places were not temples. There, the classic tragedies of bold Aeschylus, skilled Sophocles, and subtle Euripides were conceived, written, and performed.

These roots of modern theater developed gradually in classical Athens, and began as the unison singing of hymns around the altar of Dionysus, the mad wine god of frenzy and abandon. It was Thespis who first detached himself from the chorus to play out the part of the god whose deeds were being celebrated. Today, actors are called thespians.

Aeschylus added a second character, introduced dialogue, and thus reduced the importance of the chorus. Sophocles went on to add yet a third character; he increased the dialogue still further, and transformedeach play of the customary triology into an organic unit. Euripides made the characters and plots more complex by introducing social, political, and philosophical issues. He also shifted characters, who were mere pawns of Fate or divine power, to human beings in conflict in more psychological dramas.

These three playwrights (whose surviving works make up the bulk of our treasured residue of that first great age of theater) were contestants in a dramatic competition. Their official title was *tragoidoi,* a term which refers to a goat song. (The derivation of this term has been variously attributed to the fact that the original prize at these sacred festival drama contests was a goat won by the author of the best play, song; that the original chorus consisted of satyrs who wore the skins of goats, the sacred animals of Dionysus; or that the word comes from

the Dionysian attendants whose half-goat/half-man antics en-
livened the Satyr plays that offered comic relief between the
tragic triologies.)

Still, it is true that the original tragic plays are thematically
related to our later use of the term in the good fall from grace.
Tragedy is a form of literature concerned with "noble suffering," a dramatic convention which "aims at representing men
... as better than in actual life,"[4] as better than ordinary men.
Tragedy "is a paradoxical combination of a fearful sense of
rightness (the hero must fall) and a pitying sense of wrongness
(it is too bad that he falls)."[5]

The dreadful necessity of the distressing consequences of
the actions of tragic heroes are often known to them in advance. Often Fate (*deus ex machina*) seemingly serves to administer the eventual punishment, but it is the action of the
hero himself which actually leads to his being thrown by his
own weight, while "the gods are, in effect, the natural or inevitable course of things."[6]

So Fate draws the hero (or heroine) toward his (or her)
awful end by means of some "tragic flaw" of character. The
fatal weakness is most often an excess of some virtue, such as
pride or determination. The tragic hero "always gets what he
wants—and always pays the full price."[7] He appears to disturb
some natural balance which always rights itself by the final
scene. Thus tragedy tells a bit more than the truth in its exaggerated emphasis on nobility, duty, virtue, the fall of the
mighty from grace, and the inevitable restoration of natural
order.

Like the contemporary neurotic men and women who seek
my help in psychotherapy, the heroes and heroines of classical
Greek tragedy see themselves as especially selected victims of
cruel fate, made to suffer by ineluctable necessity. They feel it is
because they are somehow too good or too committed to some
inexorable higher value. They lack not self-consciousness, but
perspective and humor as they take themselves and their situations too seriously and the absurdity of life not seriously
enough. And so they cannot but participate in their own un-

happy dramatizations, yet they feel they do so through no real fault of their own.

For me Freud's most convincing counsel concerning what a psychotherapist could do for a patient is:

> No doubt fate would find it easier than I to relieve you of your illness, but you will be able to convince yourself that much will be gained if we succeed in transforming your hysterical misery into common unhappiness.[8]

Freud's point is, in part, that life by its very nature involves some frustration, pain, and disappointment. But it is not the nature of life but of neurosis that elevates such universal, everyday bits of unhappiness to the tragic extreme of "hysterical misery." The stubborn, self-willed insistence of the neurotic is not a tragic flaw of character, but a way of behaving, a solvable problem brought about by his having been too early and too often faced with more pressure and less caring than he could endure. As a psychotherapy patient, he has the opportunity to spend time in a safer, nonblaming, and yet more confronting relationship. Here he gets a second chance, in the form of an opportunity to correct earlier miscasting and to revise bad scripts. He may now learn to alternate flexibly between acting and directing, between rehearsed performances and spontaneous ad-libbing, as he increases his ability to improvise and enlarges the repertoire of his life.

Like the "tragedy" of neurotic life-style, the tragic literary convention is defined differently according to which particular scenarios are being examined. So it is that the classic interpretations of tragedy by Aristotle,[9] Nietzsche,[10] Hegel,[11] Unamuno,[12] and others, each derive from concern of emphasizing one or another of the remaining thirty-two Greek tragedies. Their interpretations and analyses differ partly in terms of the chosen drama. Because the literary convention of tragedy is a cultural phenomenon, it does *not* describe a dependable, invariant set of events. It may even be that any such term ("tragedy," the

"Renaissance," "literary realism," the "Aquarian age") is no more than a conceptual hedge, an illusion of order which we use to fend off total lunatic helplessness in the face of this overwhelmingly unordered life.

Surely my own perspective is also a biased, limited view, at least as misleading as it may be enlightening. Accepting this inevitable limitation, I will not fight against what must be but instead will try to give myself over to it openly and with gusto. Rather than try to convince you of the unlimited value of what I have to say, I will attempt to caution you (and to disarm myself) by making my biases as transparent as I can.

I wanted to write this book for many reasons. One of the fun reasons was my usual wish to get paid for opening myself to a new sort of pleasure: I got to pursue activities which my own inertia otherwise might have precluded my experiencing. (In this area I have many cop-outs. For instance, I say to myself that although I love theater, it's often too much trouble to get tickets; I somehow don't get around to buying copies of the plays I promise myself I'll read. Those slim volumes are over-priced and I often forget to return library books until they are long overdue.)

Instead I set myself up to write on psychotherapy and theater. Right off, I create the constructive distraction of appearing to gear myself to deepening my understanding of my work with patients. But beyond this lay the more private rewards of simple self-indulgence. I found myself seeing and reading many plays I otherwise would have missed. I further enriched my understanding of these delights by sampling a wide range of related writings: the history of theater, the meaning of dramatic genres, critical evaluations of many plays, performances, and playwrights; I talked with actors, attended rehearsals, and went to theater workshops. A dormant aspect of myself came to life. Again I tricked myself into becoming more alive, and I loved it!

I began by reading philosophical, historical, and aesthetic approaches to Tragedy. When possible I sampled what actors, directors, and critics had to say about them. Then I moved on to the plays. Determined to restore that discipline of mind which clears my inner vision I set out to read (or reread) every one of thirty-two surviving Greek tragedies by Aeschylus, Sophocles, and Euripides, as well as commentaries on each. Once again I was sweeping out the cobwebs of a dusty mind from the corners of my half-closed eyes.

It worked again. (It always works.) And yet I always somehow forget and let some of myself become clouded by unneeded disuse. Correcting this perennial temptation to mental lethargy is a little like taking on regular morning calesthenics, or daily periods of meditation, or ritual prayer. Just as body and spirit need regular awakening and restoring, so too does the mind. And like the others, when kept in condition this aspect of Self returns rewards far greater than the efforts reluctantly put into priming it.

And so I read the plays, some for the first time, others in a new light. I saw performances when I could. (More often though, I had to settle for listening to recordings of performances). Of these plays, one drew me back again and again, perhaps because to me it seemed the most representative of the tragic tradition—because it moved me repeatedly as theater, because the protagonists seemed caught in struggles most reminiscent of what my patients endure, because these struggles are so like my own. The play I speak of is *Antigone*,[13] the last of the Oedipus Trilogy which make up Sophocles' Theban plays, written and first performed in the city-state of ancient Athens almost 2500 years ago.

Antigone was, of course, one of the daughters of ill-famed Oedipus, who unwittingly slew his own father (Laius) and married his own mother (Jocasta). He tried to flee from a prophecy that these misfortunes would occur only to find that by his very efforts to escape he brought about the actualization of those dark forebodings. Stubbornness and prideful insistence demanded that he disclose the entire catastrophe to his unbelieving eyes.

In despair, Jocasta hung herself while Oedipus blinded

himself and asked to be banished. Antigone accompanied her father into exile. But even when she returned to Thebes after his death, her troubles were far from over. Antigone's brothers were set against one another in a terrible struggle for royal power. Eteocles held the throne and had reneged on his promise to alternate this place with his brother, Polynices. In an attempt to seize that pivotal position, Polynices and his Argive allied armies, led by seven Champions, lay seige to the Seven Gates of Thebes. After a long and bloody battle, it was decided to settle the matter in a single armed combat, a winner-take-all struggle between brother and brother. In this encounter, the sons of Oedipus killed one another. Polynices' invading hordes fled and Jocasta's brother Creon became the new King of Thebes.

Creon respected dead Eteocles as defender of his city, and so believed he should be honored. Polynices, on the other hand, assaulted his own homeland. Whatever his personal motives, Creon viewed the dead man's action as traitorous and therefore deserving of Justice so that others would be encouraged to do what was right.

He ordered the body of Eteocles be buried with honors, but issued an edict that Polynices' body "be left unburied, unwept, a feast of flesh for keen-eyed carrion birds."[14] Anyone who should defy his order was to be stoned to death.

Antigone, whose love and family loyalty once led her to accompany her blind and banished father into exile, found that she continued to love her dead brother, whatever his politics. And so, as the play begins, she is asking her sister, Ismene, to help bury their brother, Polynices, though it is against Creon's order. But Ismene does not dare join her sister in defying the law. Antigone will not be dissuaded by the threat of inevitable punishment.

Soon she is speaking to her sister with contempt. She speaks as the voice of Love, family loyalty, and natural law, setting herself over against Creon who speaks for Reason, political justice, and the gods of the State. By putting family above country (and heroism above helplessness), she sets in motion inevitably destructive forces. She is headed toward dramatic confrontation with Creon. An apparently irresistible force is about to meet a seemingly immovable object.

Willfully, she glamorizes her unyielding self-dramatization, saying to Ismene:

> Go your own way; I will bury my brother;
> And if I die for it, what happiness!
> Convicted of reverence—I shall be content
> To lie beside a brother whom I love.[15]

Hardly has Creon taken his own overstated stand when a frightened, out-of-breath sentry arrives. He reluctantly reports that someone already has dared to defy the king by scattering "dry dust over the body . . . in the manner of holy burial."[16] Outraged, Creon is quick to blame unknown citizens who disobeyed for a price or simply because they were rebellious. He ignores the cautioning voices of the Chorus. They speak with the outlook of ordinary nonheroic (and therefore, nontragic) men, telling him he may be mistaken in his stubborn decree. The overthrow of his edict might "prove to be an act of the gods."[17] They warn that:

> . . . he that, (is) too rashly daring, walks in sin
> In solitary pride to his life's end.[18]

The sentry returns with his captive, Antigone, whom he has discovered burying her brother with her own hands. Creon tries to let her off the hook by suggesting that perhaps she was unaware of breaking a punishable law. Antigone says flatly that she knew clearly that he forbade anyone to bury Polynices. Arrogantly she goes on to tell King Creon:

> I did not think your edicts strong enough
> To overrule the unwritten unalterable laws
> Of God and heaven, you being only a man.[19]

She is glad to die. It is he who is foolish. The Chorus warns that she shows her father's stubborn spirit. She too has never learned to yield. Creon answers with the moral tone of tragedy. He warns her that:

> ... The over-obstinate spirit
> is soonest broken; as the strongest iron will snap
> If over-tempered in the fire to brittleness.[20]

Glorying, martyr-like in her honorable crime, Antigone's willfulness increases. It grows exactly in proportion to her helplessness before the jeopardy in which she has put herself. The worse her situation becomes, the more spitefully she digs in.

Suspecting Ismene of complicity, Creon summons her to share Antigone's punishment. Ismene now would be glad to share the blame. Antigone rejects her sister's offer, refusing to share the spotlight with her.

Ismene pleads for mercy for Antigone. She reminds Creon that Antigone was to be married to his son, Haemon. Creon stubbornly remains the authoritarian patriarch. He is committed totally to social and political order at whatever cost of caring feelings and personal relationships. He insists that the law is *immutable*, and so Antigone *must* be executed.

Haemon goes to his father. He wishes to be the deferentially obedient son and yet is determined to plead for his beloved's life. He tries to convince his father that this trouble-making edict is unpopular with the citizenry. This simply increases Creon's anger and arrogance. It also reduces him to an attempt at a misogynous misalliance with his son expressed in his stubbornly posturing:

> Better be beaten, if need be, by a man,
> Than let a woman get the better of us.[21]

Haemon is exasperated by his father's insistent disregard for feelings. Trying to maintain his devotion to paternal authority, he urges respectable compromise. He points out that:

> It is no weakness for the wisest man
> To learn when he is wrong, know when to yield.[22]

But Creon responds by becoming even more patriarchal. He does not think of taking advice from his son, "a fellow of his age."[23] He is the King, responsible only to himself. The State belongs to him. He knows what is best for everyone. Haemon leaves in disgust telling his self-willed father:

You'd be an excellent king—on a desert island.[24]

At this point everyone is stuck and miserable. (It feels like the situations I encounter when an internecine family conflict pours over into my office for consultation. Each person is sure that things could be better, if only *someone else* in the family would give in and change. Each one wants me to make things better, to fix his broken world. My questioning of the patient's part in the mess only heightens the righteous, self-willed entrenching of his role as the heroic figure. After all, the patient's efforts to be especially good result in his being even more unappreciated. He may not be able to get his own way. At the very least, he is committed heroically to seeing to it that he will not yield to anyone else's demands.)

It is just at this point in the play that Creon begins to falter (at least in tragic terms). Though he insists on Antigone's execution, inexplicably he changes the method from stoning to entombment. This change reveals a beginning awareness of his own human fallibility. It is his subtle attempt to give Antigone another chance to discover the absurdity of her own stubborn pride. Perhaps she, too, may change her mind and give in. It is in this transformation that the plays begins to lose in tragic force and commitment to divine principles. Now it can begin to gain in humanity and appreciation of man's perennial temptation to foolishness.

If only one of the protagonists could bend perhaps neither would have to break. But in the classic tragic mode such surrender is no more likely than in its contemporary neurotic parallel. Mournfully the Chorus intones:

You are the victim of your own self-will.[25]

Both Antigone and Creon behave as though they were invulnerable and infallible. These same fictions which protect them from overwhelming feelings of helplessness and uncertainty also lead them to destruction.

Antigone suppresses any doubts she might have about her own responsibilities for her misfortunes. She projects responsibility by invoking the excuse of being a part of the ill-fated dynasty of Oedipus' family. It is like a foreshadowing of the twentieth-century Freudian cop-out: "But I had an unhappy childhood."

Now comes the entrance of Teiresias, the blind seer and therapist-in-residence. He appears to charge Creon with destructive willfulness. As consultant, he states:

> ... news you shall have; and advice, if you can heed it.[26]
> ... The blight that is upon us is your doing ...
> Only a fool is governed by self-will.[27]

He warns:

> ... Even now the avenging Furies,
> The hunters of Hell that follow and destroy,
> Are lying in wait for you, and will have their prey,
> When the evil you have worked for others falls on you.[28]

Wisely, at the point the seer does not stay to struggle with his king. He instructs by example, by doing his best, by giving in and letting go of that which he cannot control. Creon now sees the wisdom of relenting before it is too late. But it is not so easy to surrender, even to himself. He tells us what we all know and yet must relearn again and again:

> It is hard to give way, and hard to stand and abide
> The coming of the curse. Both ways are hard.[29]

Exposed as finally unheroic, Creon surrenders. Hard as it is for him to admit the error of his ways, he reverses his willful decision. He hurries off to bury dishonored Polynices and then to release Antigone. In accepting defeat and compromise, he yields to his human limitations. He tries to tolerate his hurt pride and helplessness rather than continue his heroic rush toward tragic destruction. The Chorus sings a song of praise for his putting the general well-being above his stubborn pride.

But, alas, he has yielded not too little but too late. By the time Creon reaches Antigone's tomb she has hung herself.

To the last she has gone her own way and made her own laws. Arrogantly she has refused to live whatever of this imperfect life was yet left to her. If she could not have her own way at least she could see to it that Creon did not get his way with her. In the end, Tragic heroism cannot be distinguished from commonplace spitefulness. Who commits suicide without some crypto-comic sense of self-satisfaction and smug superiority?

In classic tragic tradition, one catastrophe follows the next. This dramatic convention is as empirically unsupported as the domino theory of one catastrophe supposedly leading to another and another and another. This contemporary heroic policy position was what kept us in Vietnam for so many futile, bloody years. (If we left, all of Asia would fall and the rest of the world would follow suit. We could not leave in peace, not *without honor.* Our tragic flaw of pride would not permit us to accept our helplessness, our error, the absurdity of our principles. We ignored the necessity of giving in and going home. Our leaders would not admit that we were unheroic and no better than anyone else in that dumb play.)

In *Antigone,* the lesson is taught by Haemon's discovery that his bride-to-be has died of an out-of-hand temper tantrum. It turns out to be contagious as Haemon tries to murder his father with a sword. The old man, no longer committed to tragic heroism, is free to run to safety. In a case of mistaken identity, Haemon is reduced to killing himself instead.

His mother is not to be outdone. She decides that it is more than she can possibly bear, and so, of course, she kills herself.

Creon turns out to be the only one in the family with a sense of his own foolishness and with enough decency and humility to see that he made a big mistake. Only pathetic Creon is left with the family legacy of guilt, grief, and helplessness. Poor Creon is the only one with insight, unselfish motivation, and a willingness to change. The only decent prospect in the bunch for psychotherapy is left a wailing wreck of a man. How I would have hoped he might be able to find good counsel, learn to laugh at himself, grieve his losses, and go on to make a new life for himself.

But no! As a sixth century B.C. Greek Tragedy, our play ends with the Chorus moralizing:

> Of happiness the crown
> And chiefest part
> Is wisdom, and to hold
> The gods in awe.
> This is the law
> That, seeing the stricken heart
> Of pride brought down,
> We learn when we are old.

EXEUNT[30]

The world of Greek Tragedy is a universe ordered by divine principles. Any time that divine and human purposes conflict, the gods will be supreme. The thrust toward this inevitable consequence is set about by some man or woman who is given to heroic striving toward godliness. This gets expressed in his (or her) self-willed nature, overblown virtues, and excessive pride. A man sees himself as invulnerable, presumes himself to be most unquestionably right. Just then he is most subject to divine retaliation. The gods restore order by bringing about his tragic fall. He is sure to meet the catastrophic consequences of his prideful actions, the suffering which his inexorable fate holds in store.

The tragic hero must learn through this suffering. But all there is for him to learn is that he must live a life of moderation. His ways must not challenge higher principles. His only protection from divine retribution is to learn the humility of enduring suffering with dignity. He must come to accept the inevitability of the universal tragic moral law: the hero always gets what he wants—and he always pays the full price.

There is much to be learned from the Greek sense of man's insignificance. But the insistence that there is some higher order distresses me. They teach us something about just which attitudes bring needless unhappiness. But then they go on to insist that if only we try to be well-behaved children, that if we are good, then we may live some optimal existence in a balanced world run in accordance with the absolutely dependable principles of the wise and fair divine parents.

The contention that people often suffer as a consequence of taking themselves too seriously is played out again and again on the clasic Greek stage by the tragic hero. It is also a central theme in the consultation room of the contemporary psychotherapist, a theme with variations demonstrated by the neurotic patients who seek help.

Like Antigone and Creon, the neurotic is a person who has lost perspective, a driven creature whose actions contribute to his own needless unhappiness. The neurotic does not necessarily carry a tragic flaw of character. Yet, like the tragic hero, he suffers from an imbalance or excess of what otherwise might be virtuous, creative, worthwhile, or at least fun.

There are certain demonic qualities which, at their best, add pleasure and productivity, verve and color to our lives. Out of hand, these same lovely aspects that can be so creative can turn out to be the most destructive forces as well. I speak of sexual longing, anger, pride, the craving for power, and the like. Human strengths/weaknesses such as these are demonic in the same way as "any natural function which has the power to take over the whole person."[31] Both in the neurotic and in the tragic hero, virtues become exaggerated extensions of what they started out to be. The patient and the player become grotesque caricatures of their own initially creative thrust.

In *Antigone*, the two protagonists are exaggeratedly demonic personalities on a collision course. The play is often interpreted as a sort of allegory between religion and politics, between family ties and patriotism. This analysis can be deepened by invoking the Jungian concept of archetypes.[32]

Archetypes are inherited modes of psychic functioning which can be recognized in the recurring motifs found in man's myths and dreams, in every time and in every place.

> The familiar motifs which repeat themselves again and again in dreams and in myths include such primordial images as the original Creation, the Great Mother both as fruitful womb and as devouring destroyer, the Great Father as Lord of Heaven, wise old man, and as wrathful judge, and the Child as the link with the past. The insoluble mysteries of the relation of male and female, darkness and light, heaven and earth, the ground work of existence itself make themselves known again and again. . . .[33]

This happens via the expressions of the archetypes of the collective unconscious present in each of us.

If we do not develop self-awareness, sometimes these dark powers seem to take over. This occurs as a kind of demonic possession. Sometimes it goes so far that "people can live archetypal lives."[34] It is as though they were almost allegorical figures representing some idealized image or higher principle. All therapists are familiar with the moralistic obsessional neurotic who caricatures the ideal of duty, or the finicky compulsive whose actions both mock and honor the ideal of orderliness.

We find this with Antigone and Creon (at least to that point at which he becomes aware of what he is up to and of its terrible consequences). They are not simply two people with different ideas or conflicting needs. Each is overwhelmed by archetypal forces which direct his every action, write his every line, mold his entire character. Soon they are no longer a particular man and a particular woman arguing over opposing views of a particular situation. She becomes Woman and he, Man. Eros faces Logos. The Great Mother and the Great Father pit Feeling against Reason, Loyalty against Justice, and Conscience against Authority. The reverence of the passionate heart is dramatized into Antigone's service to the dark underworld gods of Earth. Creon elevates his obedience of the controlled mind to the carrying out of the divine order of Heaven.

The original Greek concept of the *demonic* involved a kind of dangerous ecstasy, a divine madness, well-suited to such Dionysian theatrical celebrations. The possessed person moves from a momentary state of creative inspiration to a chronic headlong plunge into a life of self-willed, stubborn archetypal immersion. That which begins as a mere fascinating dramatic highlight ends up defining the whole damn play from beginning to end.

Antigone's assertion of the principle of love begins by raising her beyond the line of least resistance. It starts by spotlighting the best of her humanity. But once she is consumed by the temptation to heroic grandeur, that same commitment to Love is exaggerated to something more than human. It engulfs her and nearly destroys her personal capacity to care for those around her. It leads her to deny the presence of love in other people.

Creon's initial interest in discovering what is fair is also willfully expanded into being dangerously more than a simple human wish to do the right thing. It leads him toward becoming a tyrannically unjust archetypal personification of the dark force of Justice. At that point, he is fair to no one, least of all to himself.

Neurotic behavior has much of this bigger-than-life, ironically self-defeating quality. Not that anyone's life should entirely lack theatrical intensity or dramatic moments. But all the world is *not* a stage, and all the men and women are *not* merely players. Life is *not* tragic, except for the neurotic. And then it is bad theater.

Theatrical performances require an audience. They are not lived for their own sake alone. So too with neurosis.

Actions on a stage are meant to be relevant to the plot. Every line reflects the character of the speaker. The audience must be entertained. There is no room for irrelevencies, repetitions, or possible boredom. But life is more random, redundant, and often more meaningless than a good play. Only for the neurotic is it as stylized, as overplayed, as tragically intense as a bad play. Surely the audience for whom any given neurotic performs will be bored unless it too has the option of participating in some reciprocal amateur production in which each can play a part. You can be in my play if I can be in yours.

But how much better I feel when I am *not* acting out some tragically heroic role. Often in recent years I am able to retain enough dramatic intensity to bring meaning to my life, to keep its performance vibrant and entertaining without having to play out the same neurotic parts for matinees and evenings without end. How much freer I feel when I am able to move beyond the tragedy of stylized, overly rehearsed actions. How much happier I am when I move beyond cliché situations supported by obviously phony props and backdrops.

More and more of the time now I realize that I need not follow certain traditional dramatic conventions. I can throw away prescribed scripts. In a world unordered by divine wisdom, I am free of parental direction, criticism, or applause. In such a world, any action is permitted.

Now consequences are somewhat predictable and yet always uncertain. The only future that is sure is that I must face the consequences of my acts, whatever they may be. In any case, I am more likely to be rewarded or punished by *how* I perform than by any good or bad reviews which others may offer.

It is an unheroic, absurdly ordinary universe, a random world without ultimate order. In such a world, no one need be typecast and all lines may be ad-libbed. What others might say does not serve as a cue line for a prepared speech. I can become more curious about what might come next. At such times I am able to move beyond the tragedy of my neurotic miscastings. At such moments, I am able to move a living theater out into the streets of spontaneity.

CHAPTER THIRTEEN

Just Pretend

Though certain kinds of pretending may lead to neurotic character styles, pretending is by no means destructive in and of itself. Without some measure of pretending, how would we escape life's uncaring harshness, its impersonal buffeting, and its tedious sameness? Creative pretending, in the form of fantasy and daydreaming, affords pleasure, excitement, relief, and even hope. Pretending can fill personal needs at times and in places in which we would otherwise have to do without. Each culture provides sanctioned ways of pretending which take people beyond the frustrations of everyday life. Such is the wonder of storytelling, the enthrallment of theater, and the grandeur of ceremony.

Pretending is the mining of the mother lode of imagination. In fantasy we may find inspiration for new ways to live. In daydreaming we may rehearse future actions so they can be approached with less fear and more grace. Reflection may even involve the practical planning which maps undeveloped projects by effectively solving problems in advance with a minimum of wasteful trial-and-error bungling.

Play is a special form of pretending. Life without play would be unbearably dreary. Being serious, realistic, and grown-up (whatever these terms mean) have their place and their own rewards. But these actions, in the absence of play, not only make Jack a dull boy, but may make him a stuffy, pompous adult as well.

Some forms of play involve solitary musings, games of self against chance, or simply isolated secret bits of whimsy which have no impact on those around us. Other kinds of play require at least one other person to be involved. This chapter will focus on this form of interpersonal play.

The communications involved in interpersonal play are by definition complex.[1] Almost all communications between people involve mood signs or signals which amend or expand the denotative implications of words and gestures. So, the tone and stance which accompany a seemingly simple salutation of, "Hey there!" determines whether we will hear it as a neutral acknowledgment, words of welcome, or an aggressive challenge.

Play requires further elaboration, another level of abstraction which brings about the mutual understanding that, "This is play!" In this metacommunication, the whole interaction is commented upon further so that I know that when you called to me so aggressively you were only horsing around, or that your very seductive tone was meant to be only flirtatious. If I misunderstand you by missing the metacommunication which would tell me that you are only playing, we may find ourselves in deep interpersonal troubles. Such misunderstandings lead to needless fights and to sticky, awkward interplays of embarrassment and hurt feelings.

Except in formal games such as sports and cardplaying the understanding that, "This is play," is not made explicit or clearly agreed upon by both parties. (Even in tennis, or in bridge, when an opponent's aggressiveness becomes "too real," he may have to be admonished to, "Remember, this is *only* a game!")

No matter how formalized or how subtly implicit, the expanded meaning of, "This is play," always implies "these actions in which we now engage do not denote what those actions *for which they stand* would denote."[2] On the tennis court, "I'm going to kill you this time!" does not imply a threat of homicide, just as at the cocktail party, "You really turn me on!" does not *necessarily* imply a sexual invitation.

Interpersonal play can be great fun, or it can be highly destructive. It is safe and rewarding to play such games if we both know that we are only playing, if neither of us is forced to play against his will, and if neither insists on changing the rules without mutual consent. We may even play exploratory games such as conversation, sex, or therapy in which the purpose of the game is to discover the rules.

Life itself may be understood as such a search to discover rules which change merely because we become aware of them. Examples range widely. In science, the von Heisenberg uncertainty principle refers to the fact that the nature of energy and matter are found to be dependent upon the way in which they are observed. Zen Buddhism teaches that there is nothing to learn, while Christianity instructs us that we may only have that which we are willing to surrender.

A contemporary drama which is made up almost exclusively of destructive interpersonal play is Edward Albee's *Who's Afraid of Virginia Woolf?*[3] The very title is a literary elaboration on a childhood game of pretend, only now it is played by adults who pretend they are too grown-up to be afraid of Big Bad Wolf.

Albee's painful comedy of bad manners takes place in the present time, in a small New England college town, in the living room of a middle-aged faculty couple. Martha is the large, boisterous, aggressively needy college president's daughter who is married to George, the sterile, passive history professor who fails to live up to anyone's expectations, even his own. They may represent a broad segment of married couples in America: they hate each other but they need each other desperately.

Together they attend a party given to welcome new faculty members. When they get home, at two o'clock in the morning, George discovers that Martha has invited a young couple over for a nightcap. Their guests are Nick, a good-looking new biology professor who turns out to be a shallow opportunist, and Honey, his mousey simpleton of a wife whom he married for her money and under the pressure of her hysterical false pregnancy. The motif of reproductive creativity, real or illusory, is also played out in George and Martha's shared fantasy of a son who does not really exist.

The four spend the next three-and-a-half hours together

drinking until they gradually strip away all the illusions which mask their ugly unhappiness. They tease and threaten each other. They fight and screw, performing ineptly in both instances. Deceitfully, they trick one another; they play games without acknowledging that they do not mean what they say, they force unwilling victims to participate in the destructive play, and they change the rules without warning. Their games include: Humiliate the Host, Get the Guests, Hump the Hostess, Bring up the Baby, and Kill the Kid.

People sometimes do play destructive games with each other. We find such descriptions in the media. Certainly this has become a popular way of describing neurotic interactions. Participants in encounter groups often are "accused" of playing games, and some schools of psychotherapy depend on this as a central concept for defining personal unhappiness and its cure. The designation of certain behaviors as game-playing is always pejorative, usually moralistic, and often implies that the person could stop if only he made up his mind to do so and tried really hard. Some therapists seem to feel that whether one plays games or is "game free" is life's only crucial issue.

Ironically, therapy may begin with trick against trick. The therapist as trickster/healer[4] introduces the *game of therapy* in order to create disinterest in the *game of neurosis*. Yet I *do not* mean to imply that the patient must lose in order for the therapist to win. My goal as therapist does not have to do with changing the patient; change is *his* goal. My purpose is to carry out the work impeccably, without regard for the results.[5] Some days I do brilliantly creative work and the patient seems to go nowhere. Other days, because I am tired, troubled, or irresponsible, I do mediocre or poor work and in response to my half-assed performance the patient is transformed and achieves new ways to happiness beyond his impatient hopes. On which days should I be satisfied: on his good days or on my own?

My use of games is merely stage magic which may distract the patient from his everyday sham. It is no more than an invitation to creative play which offers the patient the opportunity to be freed for the moment from his chronically destructive neurotic games. It is a bit like a sidewalk puppet show in a ghetto. In itself, such theater solves no problems, yet a delinquent child may become engaged in a way which promises to free his imagination so that he will be better able to solve his "real" problems.

The strategy of trick against trick is an old one. It is the "hair of the dog that bit you" and the thief you set "to catch a thief." In Tantric Yoga, it is the indulgence in passion which frees a man from passion. It is:

> A man who is poisoned may be cured by another poison, the antidote. Water in the air is removed by more water, a thorn in the skin by another thorn. So wise men rid themselves of passion by yet more passion. As a washerman uses dirt to wash clean a garment, so, with impurity, the wise man makes himself pure.[6]

The therapist's theater games are many. They include his encouraging expectations that the entire therapeutic stage is a mysterious power place in which wondrous things can happen. Like previous hits, a long run, and good reviews, the therapist's training and reputation excite hope in the patient.

His stage directions range from the simple supportively instructive suggestion that the patient's problems are familiar and soluble, to elaborate therapeutic strategies which put the patient into a double bind from which his only escape is into mental health.[7]

An example of the latter more elegant legerdemain would be the trick of dealing with frequently uncontrollable arguments between a married couple. The therapist tells them he wants them to have several fights before they meet again. If they are to be in therapy with him they must pay careful attention to every argument they have during the following week. They must each take notes on the sequence as it happens so they can present the problem for solution during the next session. If they follow the instructions to fight, they already are yielding to the therapist's control. If they pay attention and take notes, they will be fighting, but no longer in an uncontrolled way. If they choose not to fight (in order to resist the therapist's intervention) they will have made him successful in solving their problem.

Some of the therapist's games depend on theatrical props; these facilitate the patient's tricking himself into feeling how he would like to feel or doing what he would like to do. One example is the Kleenex box that lets the patient give himself the option to cry during visits to the therapist. Its obviously unobtrusive placement is beside the patient's chair; it is best if it is not beside the therapist's chair.

The analyst's couch is compellingly effective in convincing patients that they can reclaim childhood memories, associate freely, and gain more ready access to their dreams and fantasies. My own office is usually hauntingly dark and its walls are hung with primitive, mythic, and surrealistic images. Try being hardheadedly "realistic" and self-controlled in an atmosphere like that!

Still there must be different strokes for different folks. Stock properties won't always do. Sometimes new games must be invented, new props improvised. One patient had difficulty asserting herself. It was hard for her not to give in when other people demanded that she go along with their wishes rather than her own. Until her anxiety was diminished sufficiently for her to be able to fend better, I invited her to play a game with me that might help. I gave her a signed letter on my professional stationery, a "doctor's note," excusing her from submitting to other people's demands on the grounds that it would be injurious to her mental health. It worked as well as any note I ever wrote to get one of my kids temporarily excused from a physical education class!

My "game" with Ellen was more spontaneous and genuine, less hokey, but ultimately just as theatrical (in the best sense).

I liked Ellen from the first time I met her. She came to my office seeking psychotherapy, wanting help with her unhappy underestimation of herself. Nothing she did was sufficient to make her confident and no amount of affection from others could make her feel she was lovable. My feelings for her were no more to be trusted than anyone else's; they were perhaps even more suspect because of her projected overestimation of my importance.

Nonetheless, the work went well. Ellen gradually revealed herself and got to know me better. She expressed forbidden feelings, found hidden strengths, and reorganized the priorities in her life. All in all, she not only did better, but she began to feel increasingly better about who she was. Still at this point she found it hard to simply feel good from the inside, to recognize herself as a decent and lovable human being, no longer the child of uncertain worth on consignment to an approval-with-holding family.

During this second act Ellen had a very powerful set of new experiences. Through these she acquired for the first time a clear sense that she was *not* responsible for many of the awful things that occurred in her life. It was very moving for me to be with her as she came to this unburdening bit of understanding. I felt closer to Ellen and was happy for her, and I was also much encouraged by her inspired emancipation and her encouraged comradeship along the way of my own overburdened world-weary trek from out of the morass of my family scene.

At the time I had just completed my first excursion into writing; I wrote about my childhood with all of its pain, with some pathos, and hopefully with some liberating humor. I felt very vulnerable and uncertain about how effective this new sort of writing would be. It seemed suddenly right to tell Ellen about the manuscript and to expose my uneasiness about its worth to her. I offered to let her read it if she wanted to, on the condition that she not show it to anyone else.

Feeling chosen, she was very responsive. She took it home and read it with great interest. The next time I saw her, she told me how painfully compelling she found my account of my childhood struggle. She understood more clearly than ever how it was that she and I felt so close to one another. But she could not make sense why I should trust *her* with something so precious and fragile. It did make her feel worthwhile and she told me she wished she had a safe in which to put it when she got home. It was precious and for the moment she felt that she was, too. It had been a marvelous week for her; she dealt with other people with an increased ease and confidence. Yet her sense of increased self-worth obviously depended very much on the magic of having been given this splendid ritual treasure.

It was then that I told her the story of the medieval knight who attended a course at the local dragon-slaying school. Several other young knights also attended this special class taught by Merlin, the magician.

Our anti-hero went to Merlin the first day to let him know he would probably not do well in the course because he was a coward and was sure to be much too frightened and inept ever to be able to slay a dragon. Merlin said he need not worry because there was a magic dragon-slaying sword which he would give the cowardly young knight. With such a sword in hand there was no way anyone could fail to slay any dragon. The knight was delighted to have this official magic prop with which any knight, no matter how worthless, could kill a dragon. From the first field trip on, magic sword in hand, the cowardly knight slew dragon after dragon, freeing one maiden after another.

One day toward the end of the term, Merlin sprung a pop quiz on the class. The students were to go out in the field and kill a dragon that very day. The young knights rushed off to prove their mettle and in the flurry of excitement, our anti-hero grabbed the wrong sword from the rack. Soon he found himself at the mouth of a cave from which he was to free a bound maiden. Her fire-breathing captor rushed out. Not knowing that he had picked up the wrong weapon, the young knight drew back his sword in preparation for undoing the charging dragon. As he was about to strike, he noticed the change. No magic sword this, just your ordinary adequate-for-good-knights-only sword.

It was too late to stop. He brought down the ordinary sword with a trained sweep of his arm and to his surprise and delight, off came the head of the dragon!

Returning to the class, dragon's head tied to his belt, sword in hand, and maiden in tow, he rushed to tell Merlin of his mistake and of his unexplainable recovery.

Merlin laughed when he heard the young knight's story. His answer to the lad was: " I thought that you would have guessed by now. None of the swords are magic and none of them ever have been. The only magic is in believing."

Patients sometimes misunderstand the game as one in which they can believe in themselves only because I believe in them. This is a useful mistake for them to make. It gives me the power they need at a time when they mistakenly think that I am more reliable than they are. My own understanding of the game is one in which I let the patient believe in me until he is ready to believe in himself.

CHAPTER FOURTEEN

The Good Guys and the Bad Guys

There is much that seems contradictory in the life and works of playwright Bertolt Brecht: He set out to be a Communist propagandist but ended up a poet of Humanism. The non-Communist West distrusted his Communism but was enchanted by his poetry. The Communists in contrast "exploited his political convictions while they regarded his artistic aims and achievements with suspicion."[1]

The paradox in Brecht's work has to do with the unexpected results of his theory of dramatic technique, what he calls the Alienation Effect *(Der Verfremdungsefekt)*. He tried to write his plays in ways which created an atmosphere of scientific impartiality. He interrupts the action again and again so that the actors may step out of role to make didactic speeches to the audience. Props and sets are used in such a way as to keep the playgoer constantly aware that he is in the theater. It is the intent of Brecht's formalist theater techniques to discourage empathy and identification. He believed that only in this way could he hope to get across the political instruction which his plays were meant to convey.

Ironically, just the opposite is accomplished. We easily identify with the human frailty of his characters. His deliberately didactic stage techniques bring an unintended air of rollicking zaniness which prevents our taking political slogans more seriously than people.

Finally, there is the paradox of Brecht's topsy-turvy morality. He inverts the high life and the low life and switches the good guys and the bad guys in an effort to reveal how the Establishment exploits the poor and how society's dregs are victimized, forced into their seemingly destructive patterns.

The hero of *The Threepenny Opera* is Mack the Knife, a thief, a pimp, and a murderer with the habits of a burgher. He is a balding, pauchy businessman who keeps books and strives for an efficient criminal organization. In contrast the villain, Jonathan Peachum, is a pompous, moralizing solid citizen. This "legitimate" small businessman is secretly the king of beggars. He rents artificial limbs, boils, and eye patches to healthy men whom he turns out as mock cripples. Playing on the charitable impulses (read, "the guilt") of the rich who "create misery but cannot bear to see it," his business thrives. Mackie symbolizes the relationship between crime and business. Peachum "highlights the relationship between the self-seeking Capitalist ethic and the self-abnegating morality of Christianity."[2]

When I watch, listen to, or read Brecht's theater pieces, his playful switching around of the good guys and the bad guys simply makes clearer to me that *there are no good guys and no bad guys:* there's nobody here but us people.

Psychotherapists tend to think of themselves as good guys, particularly when they minister to the poor, doing long hours of treatment for relatively low wages. And yet, all therapists know that in seeking alleviation for emotional suffering, the poor get the same kind of service they always get. The help they are offered is always insufficient, often inadequate, and ultimately less geared to their needs than to those of "the good guys." As Brecht points out:

> The right to happiness is fundamental
> And yet how great would be the innovation
> Should someone claim and get that right—Hooray!
> The thought appeals to my imagination!
> But this old world of ours ain't built that way.[3]

For the most part, the therapists who service the poor in public institutions and agencies are young, inexperienced professionals; they make their beginners' mistakes on patients who can't afford the services of well-trained professionals. Many of the more seasoned therapists (those who supervise the younger therapists) are less talented, more timid, and more unimaginative members of the helping professions. Therapists who are both experienced and capable, and yet dedicated enough to stay on within the anti-therapeutic bureaucratic structures are as rare as they are valuable.

One of the many complicated yet commonplace clinic problems is the abandonment of patients. Many agencies are largely staffed by psychiatric residents, psychological interns, and social work trainees, all of whom remain at the agency no more than one or two years. The staff members who stay on long enough to develop their skills also develop the wish to work on their own. Eventually most of the more talented ones move out of the mental health agency and into the private practice of psychotherapy.

The therapist who leaves the clinic to go on with his training or to go into private practice usually feels guilty and ashamed of deserting his or her patients. In order to ease his pain the therapist may be tempted to give explanations, make excuses, or bribe the patient he is leaving behind with his good intentions and regrets. Usually the result is that the patient is then stuck with unexpressed grief and rage. It's bad enough that the patient who does not have enough money to get help in a private practice setting must endure the indignities of clinic administration, low-grade service, and cavalier dismissal; he should not have to like it as well as lump it.

The therapist plays the hidden good guy (who must appear to be the villain), a part not often played well. Try casting it. Nobody wants to play the bad guy. Here is a typical example from my experience as a therapy supervisor.

It involved a therapist I will refer to as "Dr. J." The situation would have been complicated even in the absence of Dr. J.'s need to play Jesus. As a participating therapist in one of my supervisory seminars, he chose to bring in a young patient named Marian.

Originally she went to see Dr. J. along with her husband; they sought help in resolving their marital conflict. Dr. J. saw them twice a week. After a time it became clear that Marian needed additional therapeutic space for herself. It was Dr. J.'s judgment that this should be done as a group therapy experience with a different therapist. He referred Marian to Dr. H., an excellent group therapist whose personality and approach are more detached and less mothering than Dr. J.'s and who (to complicate matters even more) had been Dr. J.'s own therapist when Dr. J. was a patient.

Over the months, Marian and her husband resolved their marital conflict by separating. Her husband left therapy. Dr. J. began to work with Marian individually while she continued to see Dr. H. in group.

Both experiences were helpful and rewarding to Marian but she began to complain that she was much happier with Dr. J. than with Dr. H. She considered Dr. H. competent, but felt pained and punished by what she experienced as his withholding.

A few weeks prior to our seminar session, Dr. J responded to her need for more help and more intense work with her personal problems. He decided and suggested that it was necessary to increase the frequency of their individual therapy to twice a week. Marian very much wanted this but said she simply could not afford to spend that much money on therapy now that she was separated and self-supporting.

In working with this therapist/patient couple in the seminar situation, I was able to identify intuitively, in a short time, the triangulation that Marian experienced with Dr. H. and Dr. J. as it related to a comparable struggle with her parents. Part of the problem in her marriage was her fantasy that she must have been drawn toward having an affair. I shared this knowledge with her; she confirmed this and painfully acknowledged that she always seemed to get involved in triangles. (I played down my role in the seminar to avoid her acting out this triangulation with Dr. J. and me as well.)

Dr. J. is a fine therapist who usually is very clear about the separation of his own role and the patient's and the necessity for a clear and straightforward contract. In this instance it seemed that he behaved differently. On the one hand, he told Marian that in his opinion, she needed to come more often for the work to go on meaningfully. When she declared that this would be a financial hardship, he tended to dismiss her economic problem in favor of suggesting that she somehow resisted going along with him for other reasons. At the same time, he simply would not say to her, "Look, this is my professional opinion. If you want to continue to work with me you have to come more often. If you cannot, then we'll have to stop." Instead, he left it open for her misinterpretation.

I suggested that he unwittingly kept Marian in a bind by giving her the impression that he was *not* saying that treatment had to be a certain way or else it must terminate. She would then be free to seek the treatment she needed through an agency that offered it at a price she could afford.

Instead, he gave her the impression that they would stay together forever. It was just a matter of negotiating a price. She hung in there and tried to be a good enough girl either to get what she wanted or to suffer enough so that he would let her have her way out of sympathy. This part of the work was clarified while Marian was still in the seminar room. After a while I suggested that she leave; the work to be done that required her participation was complete. That was agreeable to all concerned and Marian left.

Dr. J. seemed troubled and puzzled. He had been working in good faith and only now recognized the sticky bind in which he encouraged the patient to participate. With his usual show of integrity he made himself vulnerable to me and to the other therapists participating in the seminar by revealing that he felt this was an old problem of *his*, reactivated in the situation with Marian. The reason that he behaved that way had to do with his need for her confirmation that he was good and helpful. This problem came out of some early painful childhood experiences in Dr. J.'s life, a residue which arises when comparable anxieties are aroused in him from time to time.

I said: "I believe you want to be helpful and I respect that. Perhaps you can be most helpful to Marian if you are willing to do it in secret, that is without her having to know that you're being a good guy. I remember when I was last a patient in therapy. It was at a time when I struggled with a great deal of anguish over my poor health, expressed in part in the anticipatory pain of my death which would separate me from my children. While I was in therapy at that time I would speak often during my sessions of my anguish about my kids. I remember one day talking about some struggles I'd had with the kids and how good I felt about resolving them. (The kids were, at that time, teenagers and so of course there were many battles.)

"I tried to make clear to the therapist (that is to myself) how good a father I was. I told of an argument with one of the kids; I later recognized that I could have handled it a different way. I went to my son and apologized. Somehow I repaired any damage that had been done to the relationship. The therapist pointed out that it was my dependency on the kids rather than the kids depending on me about which I was worried.

"Dr. J., that's the way it is with you and Marian. You talk about how she needs you and you invite her response to that, when really you're operating out of your need for her. My therapist was very helpful at the time in pointing out that adolescence is a time for separation and that if I loved my kids, one way to show it would be to let them go. Perhaps the best way to do this would be *not* to resolve every argument but instead to let them experience me as sometimes unreasonable and cantankerous. It's hard to leave a home that feels too good. If I loved my kids I could offer them the possibility that the world outside, difficult as it might be, could be more appealing than staying, full grown, in a home with a father who sometimes was hard to get along with."

Dr. J. was responsive to what I said, experiencing my struggle with my kids as something of a mirror for his struggle with Marian. I shifted metaphors at that point. Perhaps it had to do with my recollection that Dr. J. was raised as a practicing Catholic. Athough he long since bolted the church, much that I like about him I experience as Catholicism at its best.

"Perhaps the trouble with you, Dr. J., is that you think it's better to be Jesus than to be Judas. Judas was very important. Without Judas there would have been no crucifixion, Jesus would not have been resurrected and the rest of us would not have been saved. All that was needed from Judas was that he arrange Christ's salvation of the world by being willing to be the traitor. This was to be finalized by his willingness to hang himself.

"I suppose one could argue that at least God knew what Judas was doing. After all, He'd given the assignment. If that's so, Dr. J., then you can be assured that at least God knows that you're doing the best work you can for Marian, even if you have to do it in a way that Marian herself resents. And if there is no God, if Judas' assignment was no more than his instructing himself, then Judas would simply have to settle for being good for its own sake. It's a tough business. You know what they say: 'If charity were anonymous, God pity the poor!' "

I went on to talk about some of O. Hobart Mowrer's[4] work. He did a lot of group therapy with ministers. Most of them tried hard to appear good to those around them while they hid guilty secrets inside themselves. They often ended up feeling awful about themselves.

Mowrer, himself a committed Christian, sought an answer in the history of the Church. He reminded us of the scriptural foundation for the Confessional in Jesus which bestowed upon His Apostles the authority to deal with the sins of men: "And I will give unto thee the keys of the kingdom of Heaven: and whatsoever thou shalt bind on earth shall be bound in heaven; and whatsover thou shalt loose on earth shall be loosed in heaven,"[5] and more specifically, "Whose soever sins ye remit, they are remitted unto them; and whose soever sins yet retain, they are retained."[6]

In earliest Christianity, during the first 400 years after Christ's coming, personal confession was made in public. Sins were often directed against neighbors in these small communities and so it was before the offended members that men confessed and did penance.

It was not until the fifth century A.D. that the Confessional

was sealed and sin was made a private matter between suppli-
cant and confessor. This opened the Christian community to
the forms of corruption against which Martin Luther protested. Focus shifted from confession and reconciliation with
other men to private penance and absolution. The sale of indulgences even allowed those with money to buy salvation rather
than earn it. Perhaps the most deadly consequence of sealing
the Confessional was the encouragement of everyone to play
the good guy in public, whatever his secret role.

Mowrer tells us that *we are our secrets.*[7] It is no wonder to
him that so many people live depleted lives characterized by
"neurotic" weakness, anxiety, and pessimism. Do a good deed
and we must announce it and seek immediate applause. But let
any one of us do something petty or mean and the temptation
is to hide it and even deny it if we can. Whatever bad reviews
we might have received become an accumulation of bad credits.

Mowrer's suggested remedy is to reverse the strategy, first
by admitting to the weaknesses, errors, and follies which might
make others see us as a bad guy. At the same time that we
accept the hisses and boos which divesting ourselves of these
sinful secrets might evoke from others, we must begin to try to
hide the charities, virtues, and good deeds which make us look
like we should be the ones wearing the white hats. He reminds
us of the directions given by Jesus:

> Take heed that ye do not your alms before men ... Do not sound a
> trumpet before thee, as the hypocrites do in the synagogues and in the
> streets, that they may have glory of men. Verily I say unto you, They
> have their reward. But when thou doest alms, let not thy left hand know
> what thy right hand doeth: that thine alms may be in secret: and thy
> Father which seeth in secret himself shall reward thee openly.[8]

Mowrer's contemporary translation of these directions involves his encouraging patients to confess past misdeeds in
groups (particularly in the presence of those they have mis-
treated). In addition, he urges the concealment of present and
future "good works." He goes so far as to advise patients to
stop paying fees to professional counselors; instead they are to

try admitting mistakes as they go along. The time and money they would have invested in therapy can then be used for unannounced "good works"—for what he terms "charity by stealth."[9]

Dr. J. had to decide which course to take himself. True, he could not in good conscience continue to see Marian in a treatment arrangement with sessions too infrequent to accomplish what they set out to do. Instead he could see her as often as needed without charging her more money. This would require his willingness to participate in such a charitable work; plus, he would need to work out not only what this would mean to her in the therapy relationship, but equally important, what it would mean to him. Among other considerations, he would have to acknowledge how this might further embed them both in the already sticky triangulation with Dr. H. (the good-parent/bad-parent issue).

The therapeutic situation seemed already too complicated to be beneficial to Marian if she was in some way pushed to pay more money for therapy than she could afford. She would create new problems by trying to solve old ones.

I asked Dr. J., "Are you ready, then, to set up a simple contract, making clear to Marian that the only way you'll continue to work with her is if she increases the frequency to two sessions a week?"

He said, "Sure, I've already let her know that that would be best for her."

I insisted, "No, that's not what I mean. I mean to try and make it easy for her to leave. If she can't go along with that, if she can't afford to come often enough to resolve the complexity of the therapeutic relationship then are you willing to let her go to wherever the hell she might go?"

He was taken aback. In all of this Dr. J. somehow had not quite recognized that the most meaningful therapeutic option of his might be to let her go, without her recognizing that he was doing this "for her benefit." In other words, he might help her without her knowing he was helping her.

No one wants to play the villain. But sometimes without the villain, the plot does not get developed; the story does not get told.

How much heavier the burden of the outlaw, the anarchist, or the libertine! How much more lonely to make your own way, to go on questioning everything, to say, "Yes!" to yourself and so risk everyone else saying, "No!" to you. If you are willing to forego reason and tradition rather than miss whatever might be in store for you, surely you will be classed as one of the Bad Guys.

Give way to the temptation to eat of the fruit of the Tree of Knowledge, to know it all, and then go out. Instead, we are pressured to restrain ourselves: "Be good! Don't make trouble! Go take a cold shower!" But as a committed Bad Guy, I say unto you: "Learn to give in to temptation." Ask yourself, "What do *I* feel?" "What do *I* want?" And as you begin to hear the stirrings from within, ask not, "Why?" but, "Why not?" EVERYTHING IS PERMITTED.

If we are willing to become Bad Guys, we can be guided by a contemporary immorality play by Peter Weiss. The conception is out of Brecht's interplay of many alienating levels of dramatic distance between players and audience, aimed at empowering the playwright to instruct the audience politically. But the emotional sensibility is in direct line with Antonin Artaud's Theater of Cruelty in which the play becomes "a weapon to be used to whip up man's irrational forces, so that a collective theatrical event could be turned into a personal and living experience."[10]

First produced in English almost ten years ago, Weiss' play has come to be called *Marat/Sade*. I shall refer to it here by that intimately slashed joining of the names of its two main antagonists, but not without first formally announcing its wonderfully long and compulsively accurate original title: *The Persecution and Assassination of Jean-Paul Marat as Performed by the Inmates of the Asylum of Charenton under the Direction of the Marquis de Sade.*[11]

Within the Asylum, the madmen are to put on a play-with-in-a-play. As part of their therapy, they are to enact a piece written and directed by a fellow inmate, the infamous Marquis de Sade, and perform it for an audience made up of the wealthy and privileged Director of the Mental Institution, his wife, and his daughter. The subject of the drama is the murder of Marat by Charlotte Corday during the French Revolution.

The play-within-a-play involves events which took place in 1780. *Marat/Sade* is set in 1808. And we see it now, in our own time. The Asylum audience is disturbed that under Sade's direction, the madmen may be commenting on their own times. We in turn cannot watch the production without calling into question the dehumanizing tyranny and terror of *our* present-day world. Brilliantly, the edges of reality are further hazed by the metatheatrical interplay of audience and players making nothing certain and all things possible.

> At the end of the play the asylum goes berserk; all the actors improvise with the utmost violence and for an instant the stage image is naturalistic and compelling. Nothing, we feel, could ever stop this riot; nothing, we conclude, can ever stop the madness of the world. Yet it was at this moment, in the Royal Shakespeare Theatre version, that a stage manageress walked on to the stage, blew a whistle, and the madness immediately ended. In this action, a conundrum was presented. A second ago, the situation had been hopeless; now it is all over, the actors are pulling off their wigs: of course, it's just a play. So we begin to applaud. But unexpectedly the actors applaud us back, ironically. We react to this by a momentary hostility against them as individuals, and stop clapping.[12] Standing there at the edge of the apron, virtually impinging upon the spectators, smirking sardonically, even viciously, the inmates continue to clap. Some of the audience, sensing the actors' mockery, leave quickly; some sit and wonder about the identity of the sane and the insane, and about the meaning of revolution. Sade looks on, triumphant.[13]

Today we associate the notorious name of the Marquis de Sade with the clinical terms "sadism" and "sadistic," eschewing any personal identification with such perverted psychopathological cruelty. These terms have become degrading descriptions reserved for mad-dog murderers too alien for good people like ourselves to understand. Even when used more lightly to designate disapproval of our more acceptable community members, these terms of disapprobation warn of a nastiness well beyond the limits of anything we ourselves could ever consider. Any of us might be mean or hurtful on occasion but we certainly do not enjoy inflicting pain on another human being.

And "in truth," Sade was indeed a scandalized French aristocrat arrested for brutal excesses such as whipping prostitutes in a brothel. Imprisonment led to the restriction of his active debauchery. Consequently, he funneled expression of his tumultuous desires and extreme attitudes into pornographic/philosophical writings.

Yet Peter Weiss sets Sade against Marat in his play not as pervert vs. political man, but rather as the extreme individualist against the revolutionary terrorist. Marat is the classic Marxist who wants to set rational order upon an unjust world by means of force, by being brutal *in order to* then be good to his fellow man. Knowing for sure what is right and what is wrong, Marat is a self-styled Good Guy for whom violence is a moral necessity. Had he been born in the United States in our time, he would have made a dandy Vietnam policy advisor.

Sade will not bow to "higher" moral principles and the rightness of ends justifying means. In a debate with Marat, he says:

Before deciding what is wrong and what is right
first we must find out what we are
I
do not know myself
No sooner have I discovered something
than I begin to doubt it
and I have to destroy it again
What we do is just a shadow of what we want to do
and the only truths we can point to
are the ever-ending truths of our own experience....[14]

This metatheatrical vision of Sade's led to his failure as a judge. The French Revolutionaries released him from prison and appointed him to mete out justice with the power of life and death over those he was to judge. Having fully explored orgiastic cruelty and suffering in his own imagination, he was not tempted to make others suffer in the name of some higher morality, nor could he ever impose the death sentence. He who could enjoy personal cruelty as an intoxicating excess of pleasure withdrew in horror from the State's shedding of blood as the impersonal act of murder justified in the name of Society.

What are we to make of this curious paradox of a man? He was a criminal who injured others, a pervert who scandalized the society of his time, and yet he was also a man with strong personal convictions and integrity. He was fully committed to being "thoroughly irreligious" but only in that "everything that was not human was foreign to him."[15] Ironically, his only blasphemy was against the artificial codes imposed by the impersonal collective morality of society. He wished instead only to follow Nature. Society would be tolerable only if it evolved to the point where it would forego the close-quarter tyranny of convention in favor of the reasonable anarchy of allowing individual freedom unfettered by prejudices which condemn unconventional sexual practices. In his time he was a dangerous pervert; today he would be a spokesman for the New Morality.

With prescient wisdom, almost twenty-five years ago, Simone de Beauvoir wrote an essay titled, "Must We Burn Sade?"[16] I read it again during research for this chapter and I was astounded to see just how much her vision had influenced my thinking since the time I read the piece as a young seeker so many years ago. I became aware that I was tearfully grateful to her for having given me permission *not* to need my parents' permission to be whatever I chose to be.

Part of what de Beauvoir says is that the deliberate self-corruption of the genuine libertine retains a power and a personal authenticity which is lost to the passively conforming good citizen. As he steps beyond good and evil, the libertine is free to release his imagination in the service of bringing personal meaning to his experience. The issue is *not* whether he does right or wrong, but only whether it is freely chosen and of his own decision. Sade would not rule out any desire on the basis of it being "unthinkable."

Everyone has thoughts, feelings, and acts of which he does not approve. Those who deny this must also deny the humanness of being part-ape and part-angel. Sade chose cruelty rather than indifference. He would not concern himself with what "everyone says" or what "they" do or don't do. He sought truth in personal experience. He closed no avenues, opened all doors, questioned all of Society's moral certitudes.

He freed himself from the oppression of conventional morality, from the arbitrary necessity of Right and Wrong, from the fullness of excess. He was extreme in everything. Simone de Beauvoir pointed out that this holds even in his value to the rest of us when she wrote:

> The supreme value of his testimony lies in its ability to disturb us. It forces us to reexamine thoroughly the basic problem which haunts our age in different forms: the true relation between man and man.[17]

One of the metatheatrical values of psychotherapy is that at its best, growth-oriented treatment does the same for the patients as Sade's writings do for his readers. At my best as a therapist I make no attempt to set any final goals for a patient. I really don't care what the patient does outside of the treatment relationship. Despite his attempts to invert the contract, our deal is that I run the treatment and he runs his life.

But what I do see as my side of our agreement is to help him be happier, however he defines a happy life for himself. Part of that job is to make him aware of all of his options so that he is free to choose his path and he is fully responsible for walking the way of his choice. That task involves my expert attempts to introduce him to his Shadow, to those dimensions of being human which he would disown.

The shadow is the negative side of the personality, not necessarily a bad or undesirable side, but those aspects of the self which do not fit within the idealized self-image which we each develop to make living as an imperfect human being more comfortable.[18]

I have no need for him to *live out* his shadow side, only for him to know it all. He needs to be conscious of it—not because it is necessarily valuable, but because it is his. I invite his attention to this awareness not so that he will change his life but only so that he comes to know he could.

This introduction to the hidden "bad guy" came about recently in therapy. I have been working with a young woman for over a year in what has been essentially a rewarding and productive relationship for both of us. She has, however, always been somewhat low-keyed in the expression of her feelings. Particularly there has been very little direct show of anger by Sally. When she is resentful she is more likely to express some sense of hurt or of dissatisfaction *with herself.*

She has been living with a man for some months. This relationship is one that they both enjoy, although it has quickly tapered off from being an intense love relationship to what she describes as more of a brother-sister relationship. They enjoy each other's company. They share many activities but she admits that often she has feelings of dissatisfaction about the relationship which she does not express directly.

Along with this she also now is complaining that she seems largely to have lost interest in their sexual activities. She sometimes participates more or less "for him," but most often simply declines because she does not feel like having sex. It is a puzzle for her that most of the time when they do have sex, she enjoys it. The problem seemed to be an unrecognized power play involved in the initiation of sex between them.

She describes her lover as quite aggressive. He almost always approaches her (although when she is disinclined he accepts her excuses). Because he is always ready to approach her, she explains to herself that she never has to initiate sex by being seductive or sexually demanding in any way.

In a recent meeting with Sally, I made a therapeutic error toward the end of the session. It occurred during the closing minutes of the hour. She began what I thought was going to be a brief final comment on what we discussed. Instead, it turned out that she initiated a long and complicated story which was related to what we had been talking about up to that point.

I interrupted, but did not do it cleanly. That is, I should have said simply, "Our time is up." Instead, I interrupted by saying, "I thought you were simply about to make a comment on what you had been saying. Now I realize that you have begun a story which you won't have time to finish because it's the end of the hour. So rather than let you get started and then have to interrupt you we'll just stop now."

She left the hour without further comment.

Shortly after this Sally began to express concern about the physical problems she knows I have in retaining my balance. Setting about to "take care of" me, she proposed that she not require my coming to the waiting room to get her at the start of each appointment. (I usually listen to music between sessions. It's my practice to turn off the sound system just before I head to the waiting room to get the next patient.) What she began to do was listen for the music to be turned off and then pop out of the waiting room just as I was coming to the door—"to save me the trouble" of coming to get her. Ironically, this attempt to protect me from losing my balance usually threw me off balance; it startled me as she came out of the waiting room without warning. Recognizing this, Sally laughed embarrassedly about it. In the hallway, at first mistakenly seeing all of this as outside of the therapeutic context, I simply said to her, "Do me a favor: don't do me any favors."

Sally herself is a practicing psychotherapist. In a subsequent hour she expressed some distress about how some of her patients responded to her no-smoking rule in the group she leads. Their response to her *interrupting* their smoking came in the openly angry form of contempt and verbal abuse of the sort that she herself would never express.

I interpreted this account as an unconscious derivative arising from the adaptive context of the unfinished transaction in which I ineptly interrupted her. She responded with no show of feelings, but soon began to be "good" to me in a way that I experienced as assaultive. She responded to my interpretation by relating her preoccupation with the way her patients reacted to her interrupting their activities; she acknowledged that she herself developed somewhat resentful feelings in response to the way that I interrupted her story at the end of the earlier session. She complained mildly that I had done it in a way that seemed to inhibit her from feeling angry and showing it.

As is my custom, I immediately confessed (that is, I admit to whatever patients accuse me of doing, and then I explore it with them). As we continued to explore the incident, I commented on how inhibited she *still* was about her annoyance at being dealt with this way. In response she admitted that at some point she'd had a disturbing fantasy. She could not quite claim it as her own, but rather described it as a thought which just kind of came into her head. She said it was something about having thought for a moment of punching me in the head. She felt guilty and greatly upset by having had such a thought.

This is very unusual material for this woman, the sort of feeling which does not fit at all well with her usual self-image. I encouraged her by treating her admission of this fantasy as an act of trust in our relationship: she felt safe enough to tell me she thought of doing something so terrible to me. Elaborating on this fantasy a bit she said that she knew her image of my head was one of fragility, like a baby's head (because of the intracranial surgery which I had undergone). She pointed out that she thought of punching me, not in the mouth, but in the head. She felt that my mouth, which had interrupted her, was strong and hard to fight while my head was weaker and more vulnerable.

She was quite upset at having had such a thought and did what she could to discredit it. With some urgency she disassociated herself from evil, insisting that she was just not the sort of person who had such thoughts.

I responded by acknowledging that she certainly did not think of herself, nor did she usually act like that sort of person. And yet I told her that somehow, intuitively, I felt there were more sadistic fantasies that went with her elaborations of the associated bad thought. She thought about it quite seriously and replied, "No, I never have sadistic fantasies." And again, "I guess I'm just not that sort of person.

I suggested to her that while that was clearly not how she experienced herself, it might be useful for her if, for a moment, she could stand it to *pretend* that she *was* the sort of person she really was not. The idea seemed to appeal to her so long as we both understood she was only pretending and that she was *not* acting out the part of who she *really* was.

Once she let herself into that space she confirmed my interpretation by coming up with some fresh childhood memories. She told of the fun she used to have as a little girl when she cut up worms and watched how long they wiggled and squirmed before they died. She allowed herself this sadistic pleasure for just a short while as a little girl. Soon she generalized from the family miscasting directive as to what sort of person she was allowed to be. It required that she feel there was something wrong with her if she could enjoy herself without feeling bad about the suffering worms. Her part called for her to feel that it was unkind; how the worms must be suffering! She began to feel so extraordinarily guilty that soon she had to give up even thinking about doing such things. On that day it was worms, the next day it could be her parents.

I expressed delight that she could remember a time when, like the rest of us, she enjoyed the power of being gratuitously cruel. Something about this exchange led her to some thoughts about her love relationship. I suggested that there were comparable feelings underlying her troubled sexual relationships. Her first response was the defensive denial which family pressure had earlier required she establish. Her script did not allow sadistic fantasies toward loved ones. She said no, it's not at all true, in fact, she very much regretted *not* having sexual feelings about the man with whom she lived. Indeed she was quite concerned that he would feel bad about her sexual unresponsiveness.

Again I asked her to pretend that she was not the sort of person she really is, but rather that she imagine herself to be the sort of woman who might get sadistic pleasure out of withholding sex from a man. She began to smile mischievously. It took her a while but with some encouragement on my part she could admit that: "If I were *that sort of woman,* I can imagine the enjoyment in seeing a man be very horny—squirming and pleading—when he wanted sex and couldn't get it."

Suddenly she knew that she was that sort of woman as well. She could now own the unconscious fantasy she had been having about her "unfortunate" disinterest in sex with her boyfriend.

Sally moved from that material to a more open expression of closeness and affection for me and was much more expressive in what she had to say about the pleasure of those feelings than she had been previous to that point. I suggested to her that we were reliving some of what she was going through with her boyfriend and that she had gone through with her parents. That is, the rule of thumb for her life with her boyfriend might be, "If you don't fight, you don't fuck." So long as she insisted on casting herself as the sort of person who was acceptable to her parents, who could not even think of being resentful in a cruel or vindictive manner, then she would have to bury full expression of her affection and closeness along with those denied bad feelings of sadistic anger.

She seemed uneasy and yet encouraged by the recognition of her expression of sadistic fantasies toward me and began to tolerate the conception that she indeed was the sort of person who could have any sort of fantasies no matter how unacceptable they were to her parents. When she accepted her shadow side then she also could be a more loving, passionate, emotionally expressive human being than she had been since the time she was a very little girl.

CHAPTER FIFTEEN

Make It Up as You Go Along

How then are we to gain the freedom to improvise? First we must learn to give up our studied, well-scripted, often miscast, bigger-than-life tragic roles.

The original tragic heroes of classic Greek theater literally were outsized representations of exaggeratedly more-than-human proportions, very special sorts of characters. Inflated in top-heavy, traditional padded robes, their natural height was enlarged grotesquely by ornamental headdress (*Onkos*) and by the thick soles on their high boots (*Cothurni*). To the artificial magnificence of their high-soled boots was added face masks that at the same time identified the characters and served as megaphones! Surely their style of performance was as high-flown as their costuming.

It is so easy to be tempted to remain stuck in a limited life role which offers little reward beyond its safe sense of familiarity. No matter how dangerous the consequences of staying in character, each of us sometimes is tempted to live out his tragic role rather than risk a new part or an unfamiliar, who-knows-what-will-happen-next improvisation.

A patient of mine was stuck in this way, fearful of reaching for the freedom to improvise. Karen was the daughter of a drunken, suicidal father and a saccharine, feeling-denying mother. As a result, she spent much of her adult life seeking to become the loved little girl she missed as a child. The price was exorbitant. She tried hard to please and when someone found her acceptable she felt high on the fantasy that she was a good little girl loved at last. But at those times when she could not arrange to be the object of someone else's approval she felt as desperately lost and alone as when she was growing up in that awful house so long ago.

After some experience in therapy, Karen could see that in order to leave behind her the dreadful depression of being a lost little girl, she had to give up the ephemeral fantasied rush of being a loved little girl. She saw the choice but still she hesitated.

In order to illustrate the irony of her dilemma, I told her of the classic piece of business which comedian Jack Benny made famous. Years ago on his radio show, there was an episode in which Mr. Benny walked alone down a dark street. The radio audience knew that the stock-in-trade of his comic character was his studied miserliness. And so audience tension was high when Mr. Benny was confronted by a street marauder whose sullen voice demanded, "Your money or your life."

The demand was followed by Mr. Benny's silence.

Again the mugger insisted, the threatening harshness of his voice growing louder, "I said, 'Your money or your life!' "

Again, Benny's silence.

"For the last time," the mugger shouted. "Your money or your life!"

Another brief silence, and Mr. Benny whined, "I know, I know! (long pause) I'm thinking it over."

Even the most natural improvisations become unavailable in someone who has been oppressively miscast in an overly scripted life. Sometimes it is necessary to remind patients that there must have been some time in their lives when they reached out because they felt loving, shouted when they felt angry, and cried when they hurt. Such people feel so locked into prescribed roles that even though they cannot deny that as young children they must have once felt free to do as they pleased, they cannot remember ever having had that freedom; all they know now is that it is forbidden to improvise.

Arthur Schopenhauer recounts a theater story which captures the flavor of such cruelly stilted direction. He tells:

... of an actor, called Unzelmann, who was rebuked by his director and colleagues for too much improvising. One day Unzelmann appeared in a play that demanded his presence on stage with a horse. During the performance the horse dropped something natural to the horse, but unbecoming and unusual in the midst of a scene. The audience roared with laughter. Unzelmann turned to the horse and said: "Don't you know we are forbidden to improvise?"[1]

Even when people realize that they are allowed to change and to do as they please, they may be afraid that they will not be able to handle new situations. Psychotherapy patients, like the rest of us, are of course understandably reluctant to give up roles in which they feel competent and confident for the uncertainty of future improvisation.

When a patient struggles with such a problem, I sometimes tell him the story about my son Nick's feelings of dread as he anticipated sixth-grade mathematics.

He was in fourth grade at the time, his next oldest brother in sixth grade. Nick listened to David talk about his own work in that term's sixth-grade math. Nick commented uncomfortably: "I'll never be able to do that kind of homework."

I assured him that he certainly would be able to do it when the time came. Nick's poignant response was, "Don't be silly, Dad. How could a fourth-grader handle sixth-grade math?"

The therapist must be careful not to help too much when the patient is anticipating his own handling of sixth-grade math. He must remember the story of the boy who, out of compassion, tried to help free an emerging butterfly from its sticky cocoon. The butterfly got out but immediately fell helplessly to the ground; it was unable to fly. Fortunately, the boy's father was there to explain that the struggle to emerge from the sticky cocoon is precisely what is needed to strengthen the butterfly's wings, enabling it to fly once it is free. The boy then understood that in doing the butterfly this favor, he had done it no favor.

Even when we feel able to cope with new ventures, our vision of ourselves in relation to our audience may lead us to resist going on to new ways of acting. How often we struggle against improvising new roles even when it is clearly to everyone's advantage that we do so. The changing roles invited by the Women's Liberation Movement offer many poignant examples, some funny, some sad, some a bit of each. A peculiar instance arose recently in the North Carolina State Legislature in which the Equal Rights Amendment was defeated. It had been passed one day by preliminary vote only to be defeated the next in the final tally by two last-minute vote switches:

> One changed vote was that of a woman, Representative Myrtle E. (Lulu Belle) Wiseman, who tearfully explained later that her switch was caused by a flood of phone calls from friends and neighbors back home in Avery County.
>
> "I know they don't know what ERA is all about," Mrs. Wiseman was quoted saying to all the press services, "But I just couldn't in my own heart vote against my people."[2]

So she voted against herself instead.

There may be helpers along the way, but other people's expectations often turn out to be more of a hindrance than a help. In the long run, the freedom to improvise often requires that we give up hope of having an appreciative audience. Often the onlookers are too ready to ask that we do it some other way than our own, that not our will, but theirs be done. I've seen friends get their things together, change "serious" roles for the fun of improvising, only to be met with criticism instead of pleasurable appreciation that their new happiness might understandably inspire. That's how it was for Salik.

I met Salik during one summer vacation on Cape Cod. For years he was a very successful practicing psychoanalyst in New York City. It was on a vacation of his own that he found the freeing experiences which ultimately allowed him to give up the studied role which his middle European Jewish culture had dictated and to take on a scary but exciting life of daily improvisation. Salik went to Haiti for just three weeks. There he met a beautiful black butterfly of a woman, a Haitian actress and primitive painter.

Salik himself had long loved to paint. But his official role necessitated his reducing this first love to nothing more than a hobby.

By the time his Haitian vacation grew near the end, the two knew they loved each other. For a few days they played at plans about how they would get together again in the future. But at last Salik realized this was empty fantasy. If he left her now, that would be the end.

Instead they decided to marry then and there. His wife returned to New York with him to help him close down his practice, to gather up what little money they both had, and to move toward redefining their own lives in terms of doing what was most important to each of them: painting. They tried to figure out how long they could live on the little money they had and the bit more they expected to make. Salik told me that their working plan was to count on spending $4,000 a year for necessities, and another $4,000 for incidentals.

By the time I met them they had been married for several years and had three beautiful children. They were living six months out of the year in a house on Gull Pond on the Cape and the other six months in Cuernavaca, Mexico. When I asked how difficult it was for the children to shift back and forth between an English-speaking country and a Spanish-speaking country, they laughed. It turned out they all spoke French at home and ad-libbed in whatever community they found themselves.

Salik himself had become a satisfyingly successful colorist after a while. That summer Marjorie and I bought from him a large canvas in powerful intensities of dark mottled yellows and astonishing floods of red.

As we got to know each other Salik told me of the confusion in the audience that came as he switched roles. After being away from New York for a while, his painting began to get some recognition. His agent told him that a one-man show of his work was being arranged in New York. He went back to the city for the first time in many months to help make the show all that he hoped for.

He contacted some of his old psychoanalyst friends. They

were delighted to hear from him and arranged a party. They showed great pleasure in welcoming him back and they all offered to help him open a new practice and restore him to his true role.

Salik was grateful but assured them that he was happy and successful as an artist. The party broke up early. None of the other analysts ever called him again. Finally, he realized that they had only been happy to see him because, mistakenly, they were sure he was returning because he had failed.

Salik's story was recently brought to mind again by the improvisation of another friend. Gary is the president of a social-problem-solving company. Recently he discovered quite another sort of pleasure in his life: Gary has begun to bake wonderful loaves of bread. He loves working with the dough, baking, the hot sweet-smelling loaves, eating them, and giving them to his friends. He has begun to take off two or three afternoons a week from his role as president of the company in order to stay at home and bake.

Someone from out of his past was in town for a conference. She called Gary, visited him and his wife, and inquired with interest about his latest accomplishments. When he spoke in his moving way about his newfound delight in being a baker, she wasn't sure exactly how to respond. Unfortunately, she recovered her poise by replying that that was really wonderful for Gary because his descriptions of the aesthetic and sensual pleasure of kneading the dough made it clear to her that he was on his way to becoming a sculptor!

We must learn to maintain a freedom to improvise parts for ourselves guided by inner wishes and to our own pleasure, rather than by what our audiences have in mind. Another friend helped make me even more aware of this struggle.

Toby is a jazz pianist, composer, and music teacher who comes from an Ivy League, accomplishment-oriented family. This made for some family resistance when as a teenager he chose to go to a music conservatory instead of a "real" college.

Toby gave himself to studies at the conservatory as fully as he gives himself to anything else that intrigues him. When he learned as much as he thought the conservatory had to teach him, he of course left to work things out for himself. It was years later that he learned that his family considered this move —from the formal role of music student (which they had begun to accept) to that of improvising musician—as a mark of his failure as a dropout.

As a performing art, music has always seemed particularly instructive to me as a model for what a freely improvised life can be like. I remember reading one musician's description of when he gave up playing the recorder to learn to play the flute. On the first instrument he played competently in a well-trained but timid style. The flute was frightening but it opened him to a new freedom of improvisation. Here is how he described the experience:

> Wandering over the unfamiliar terrain of a new instrument, my fingers broke free of their recorder habits, to new rhythms and patterns, reflecting what I'd heard but born from the moment. I could wave them *freely* —not always, but enough at times to express what was in me. Sometimes still, jamming with others, when I am down or ill at ease, I can hear myself "going through the motions," appearing to make music in a whole when actually my mind is checking off the chord changes and dragging familiar licks out of storage for my fingers to permute. But if we start cooking together, I can feel almost a click in me as another *system* takes hold in response, and energy flows from within through my fingers, which leap their baroquish walls to skitter across the keys, chasing the wind.[3]

He goes on to explore the experience of allowing himself this freedom:

> What are the traps? If I am anxious for the next note, or about it, I do not listen to the one I am in. *Be where I am.* If I am anxious to hang on to the goodness of where I am, for fear any change may make the note more sour, my body translates this into frozen fingers and lips that cannot move. *Don't be afraid to let go; learn to have nothing to lose.* To move in holy indifference is not to be passive....[4]
>
> Yet sometimes the music itself leads me forth, embracing even my tremors and contradictions in something whole. Playing free, every so often I realize that the note I have just begun is not the one "I" had

intended and sent out orders to produce, but a different one chosen confidently by my body to extend the music—quite independently of the listening-and-scheming me who flashes with resentment at the *mistake.*

My instruction by this man was expanded by another highly creative musician. Toby and I together went to see the Bill Evans Trio perform at a Smithsonian Institution Jazz Concert. (Evans is a player and composer who has reharmonized the piano for a generation of jazz players.) The trio consisted of himself, a bass player, and a drummer. Unlike most other such trios, these men seemed in many ways equally matched. In most numbers the other players are featured for solos; they don't serve merely as a setting for Evans' piano playing. The bassist, Eddie Gomez, performed remarkably lyrical improvisations in his seemingly unlikely instrument. The bass is usually the equivalent to the Oriental drone, which offers persistent background rhythm and not much in the way of melody or ideas. The drummer, Marty Morrell, is best described by Evans himself when he says, "If Marty were playing with a feather there would still be fire in his touch."

Before the evening concert, there was a jazz workshop in the afternoon. The trio offered a brief informal concert and then left themselves open to questions from the audience. This is an extremely hazardous thing to do in that it invites a great deal of ego-tripping and expression of resentment born of envy when the otherwise adoring audience is given a chance to switch itself into performance roles.

Nonetheless, Evans fielded the questions with grace, poise, and intelligence. His low-keyed, slow-moving subtle wit was not an easy target for the barbs which he encountered.

Question: "In what direction are you headed musically, Mr. Evans?" Answer: (long thoughtful pause) "What direction am I headed in? I would say .. *down* ... and, of course, ... *in!*"

Evans then went on to explain something about deepening his sense of what he is doing. He always follows his own direction rather than collective trends. He works hard to master some mode of music, some working of the chords. He works, and works, and works, and works, until finally that aspect of the music is available to him "at an unconscious level."

But he warned that once you get something that well in hand, you have to be very careful not to become lazy and fall into it rather than take each new moment of music and do something immediate in response to it.

At that point someone else asked him, "How often do you work out in advance any improvisation you may play within a given performance?"

Evans' answer was, unhesitating: "Never!"

Another question: "I've been a musician for twenty years but I still can't improvise. How do I get a feeling for jazz?"

Evans' answer: "Practice!"

Freedom to improvise requires a radical shift from familiar patterns, risking the displeasure and discouragement of the audience. It means giving up familiar pain for unfamiliar pain. Sometimes it requires being able to laugh at oneself and endure the ridicule of others. Often it requires hard work. Other times it demands that we give up working hard so that we may begin to play.

And even if I do give up old roles and get beyond old problems, some of my new routines might be as hokey as my old ones. I have spent so much time fooling other people I sometimes end up fooling myself. The dangers are perhaps particularly great in the current setting of our countercultural, encounter group, mystical-occult Aquarian Age, where there are ready-made mass-media modeled costumes, props, and lines for the new free spirits, for those of us who would be the contemporary improvisers. Recently I came across a delightful Zen-on-Zen story, a helpful cautionary reminder for guarding against my own predilection for such stereotyped stylish solutions.

Traditionally Zen monasteries will only admit wandering Zen monks if they can show proof of having solved a *koan*.

It seems that a monk once knocked on a monastery gate. The monk who opened the gate didn't say "Hello" or "Good morning," but "Show me your original face, the face you had before your father and mother were born." The monk who wanted a room for the night smiled, pulled a sandal off his foot and hit his questioner in the face with it. The other monk stepped back, bowed respectfully and bade the visitor welcome. After dinner host and guest started a conversation, and the host complimented his guest on his splendid answer.

"Do you yourself know the answer to the *koan* you gave me?" the guest asked.

"No," answered the host, "but I knew that your answer was right. You didn't hesitate for a moment. It came out quite spontaneously. It agreed exactly with everything I have ever heard or read about Zen."

The guest didn't say anything, and sipped his tea. Suddenly the host became suspicious. There was something in the face of his guest which he didn't like.

"You *do* know the answer, don't you?" he asked.

The guest began to laugh and finally rolled over on the mat with mirth.

"No, reverend brother," he said, "but I too have read a lot and heard a lot about Zen."[6]

An Eschatological
Laundry List:

A Partial Register of
the 927 (or was it 928?)
Eternal Truths

The compiling of my Laundry List happened during one of those uncluttered spaces when I took time out to enjoy the pleasure of writing to a loved friend far away, an unobligated letter born wholly out of abundance.

The subject of this particular letter was the foolishness of pontificating in my profession.

So it was that I came to include in this letter a list of "Eternal Truths." I did not have to search for them. They arose from my unconscious as in a dream, taking form almost more quickly than I could write them down. This was to be a zany private spoof, a way of tenderly making fun of myself. Instead, what emerged was a fragment of a cosmic joke, a visionary list of truths which, at my best, shape my life, provide answers to unasked questions, and gives insights too powerfully simple to be grasped finally and forever.

I, of course, was at first too "wise" and too rational to take all of this seriously. This list was for me a mere bit of play, a throw-away piece.

My decision to try to get it published was itself a lark. I titled this piece of guru-correspondence "An Eschatological Laundry List: A Partial Register of the 927 (or was it 928?) Eternal Truths," and submitted it to *Voices* (my favorite psychotherapy journal).

Not only was it accepted for publication, the readers loved it! I received letters of request for as many reprints as I could spare. People often had their own items to add to the List. Some compile their own personal lists; others asked me for a copy of the remaining 884 (or was it 885?) Truths. It did not seem to matter whether people took the list seriously or found it funny—somehow it spoke to them. Laura Popenoe, an artist I'd met, urged me to let her make a poster of the list. Thousands of people bought copies of the list, hung it on the walls within which they lived or worked. It was the first piece of my writing to become something to live with. I could hardly believe how much more response I had evoked with this gratuitious plaything than with some of my "more serious creative efforts".

1. This is it!
2. There are no hidden meanings.
3. You can't get there from here, and besides there's no place else to go.
4. We are already dying, and will be dead for a long time.
5. Nothing lasts!
6. There is no way of getting all you want.
7. You can't have anything unless you let go of it.
8. You only get to keep what you give away.
9. There is no particular reason why you lost out on some things.
10. The world is not necessarily just. Being good often does not pay off and there is no compensation for misfortune.
11. You have a responsiblity to do your best nonetheless.
12. It is a random universe to which we bring meaning.
13. You don't really control anything.
14. You can't make anyone love you.
15. No one is any stronger or any weaker than anyone else.
16. Everyone is, in his own way, vulnerable.

17. There are no great men.
18. If you have a hero, look again; you have diminished yourself in some way.
19. Everyone lies, cheats, pretends (yes, you too, and most certainly I myself).
20. All evil is potentially vitality in need of transformation.
21. All of you is worth something, if you will only own it.
22. Progress is an illusion.
23. Evil can be displaced but never eradicated, as all solutions breed new problems.
24. Yet it is necessary to keep on struggling toward solution.
25. Childhood is a nightmare.
26. But it so very hard to be an on-your-own, take-care-of-yourself-cause-there-is-no-one-else-to-do-it-for-you grown-up.
27. Each of us is ultimately alone.
28. The most important things, each man must do for himself.
29. Love is not enough, but it sure helps.
30. We have only ourselves, and one another. That may not be much, but that's all there is.
31. How strange, that so often, it all seems worth it.
32. We must live within the ambiguity of partial freedom, partial power and partial knowledge.
33. All important decisions must be made on the basis of insufficient data.
34. Yet we are responsible for everything we do.
35. No excuses will be accepted.
36. You can run, but you can't hide.
37. It is most important to run out of scapegoats.
38. We must learn the power of living with our helplessness.
39. The only victory, lies in surrender to oneself.
40. All of the significant battles are waged within the self.

41. You are free to do whatever you like. You need only face the consequences.
42. What do you know ... for sure ... anyway?
43. Learn to forgive yourself, again and again and again and again.

Notes

Chapter 1

1. Joseph R. Royce, "Metaphoric Knowledge and Humanistic Psychology," *Challenges in Humanistic Psychology*, ed. James F. T. Bugental (New York: McGraw-Hill, 1967), p. 27.
2. James Dickey, "Metaphor as Pure Adventure" (Lecture delivered at the Library of Congress, Washington, D.C., 1968), p. 2.
3. Susanne K. Langer, *Philosophy in a New Key* (New York: New American Library, A Mentor Book, 1952), p. 120.
4. Owen Thomas, *Metaphor and Related Subjects* (New York: Random House, 1969), p. 4.
5. Langer, *Philosophy in a New Key*, p. 119ff.
6. Dickey, "Metaphor as Pure Adventure," p. 9.
7. Langer, *Philosophy in a New Key*, p. 111.
8. Ibid., p. 164.
9. Ibid., p. 228.
10. Dylan Thomas, *The Collected Poems* (New York: New Directions, 1953), p. 15.
11. Ibid., pp. 194ff.
12. Ibid., p. 124.
13. Henry M. Pachter, *Paracelsus: Magic into Science* (New York: Henry Schuman, 1951), p. 63.
14. Dickey, "Metaphor as Pure Adventure," pp. 12ff.
15. M. H. Abrams, *The Mirror and the Lamp: Romantic Theory and the Critical Tradition* (New York: W. W. Norton & Co., 1958), p. 57.
16. Vincent F. O'Connell, "Until the World Become a Human Event," *Voices* 3 (Summer 1967): 75–80.
17. Arnold J. Toynbee, *A Study of History*, 2 vols. (New York: Dell Publishing Co., A Laurel Edition, 1:288.
18. Leonard Cohen, "Suzanne Takes You Down," *Selected Poems, 1956–1968* (New York: Viking Press, A Viking Compass Book, 1968), p. 209.
19. Erich Fromm, *The Forgotten Language, An Introduction to the Understanding of Dreams, Fairy Tales and Myths* (New York: Rinehart & Co., 1951).
20. Ibid., p. 33.
21. *Oxford English Dictionary*, 1961, s.v. "charisma."
22. I Cor. 13:1.

23. Ibid., 13:2.
24. Ibid., 14:2.

Chapter 2

1. Elie Wiesel. *One Generation After,* Translated by Lily Edelman and the author, Bard Books/Published by Avon, New York, 1972, pp. 94ff.
2. C. C. Jung, Review of G. R. Heyer, *Praktische Seelenheilkunde. Zentralblatt fur Psychotherapie,* IX (1936, 3: 184–187). Coll. Works, final vol. Quoted in *Psychological Reflections; An Anthology of the Writings of C. G. Jung,* selected and edited by Jolande Jacobi, Harper & Row, Publishers, New York, 1961, p. 68.
3. Archibald MacLeish, "Hypocrite Auteur," *Collected Poems 1917–1952,* Houghton Mifflin Co., Boston, 1952, p. 173.
4. Alan Watts. "Western Mythology: Its Dissolution and Transformation," in *Myths, Dreams, and Religion,* Edited by Joseph Campbell, A Dutton Paperback, E. P. Dutton & Co., Inc., New York, 1970, p. 14.
5. Joseph Campbell. "Mythological Themes in Creative Literature and Art," in *Myths, Dreams, and Religion,* (1970), pp. 138–175.
6. James Joyce. *Ulysses,* Random House, New York, 1934, p. 574.
7. C. G. Jung. *The Archetypes and the Collective Unconscious,* from the Collected Works of C. G. Jung, Volume 9, Part 1, Bollingen Series XX, Princeton University Press, Princeton, New Jersey, Second Edition, 1968.
8. Ibid. p. 183.
9. C. G. Jung. "Wotan," *Neue Schweizer Rundschau* (N.S.), III, 11, (Mar., 1936: 657–69. In *Coll. Works,* Vol. 10, p. 12). Quoted in Jacobi, p. 36.
10. Martin Buber. *Moses: The Revelation and the Covenant,* Harper Torchbooks, Harper & Row, Publishers, New York, 1958, p. 17.

Chapter 3

1. Ibid., p. 102.
2. Philip G. Zimbardo, Paul A. Pilkonis, and Robert M. Norwood, "A Shrinking Violet Overreacts: The Social Disease Called Shyness," *Psychology Today* 8 (May 1975): 72.
3. T. S. Eliot, "The Love Song of J. Alfred Prufrock," in *Collected Poems 1909–1935* (New York: Harcourt, 1930), pp. 11–17.
4. Guy de Maupassant, "The Diamond Necklace," in *The Best Stories of Guy de Maupassant,* ed. Saxe Commons (New York: Random House, 1945).
5. Ibid., pp. 241–242.
6. Ibid., pp. 242–243.

Chapter 4

1. Lewis Carroll. *Alice's Adventures in Wonderland* and *Through the Looking-Glass,* with all the original illustrations by Sir John Tenniel, Macmillan, London, Melbourne, Toronto, St. Martin's Press, New York, 1968, p. 48.
2. Erving Goffman. *Relations in Public: Microstudies of the Public Order.* Basic Books, Inc., New York, 1971.

3. a. Robert Ardrey. *The Territorial Imperative: A Personal Inquiry into the Animal Origins of Property and Nations,* a Laurel Edition, Dell Publishing Co. Inc., New York, 1971.
   b. Goffman (1971).
   c. Edward Hall. *The Hidden Dimension.,* Double Day, New York, 1966.
   d. Konrad Lorenz. *On Aggression,* Bantam Books, Inc., New York, 1967.
   e. Lionel Tiger and Robin Fox. *The Imperial Animal.* Holt, Rinehart and Winston, New York, 1971.
4. William Golding. *Lord of the Flies.* Capricorn Books, G. P. Putnam's Sons, New York, 1959.
5. Anna Freud and Dorothy T. Burlingham. *Infants Without Families.* Medical War Books, International University Press, New York, 1944.
6. Colin Turnbull. *The Mountain People.* Simon and Schuster, New York, 1972.
7. Philip G. Zimbardo. "The Psychological Power and Pathology of Imprisonment," *Selected Documents in Psychology,* MS. NO. 347, American Psychological Association Journal Supplement Abstract Service, Washington, D.C., 1973.

Chapter 5

1. A. A. Milne, *Winnie-the-Pooh* (New York: E. P. Dutton & Co., 1926, 1954), p. 38.
2. Ibid., pp. 40ff.
3. Ibid., p. 28.
4. L. Frank Baum, *The Wizard of Oz* (Chicago: Reilly & Lee Co., 1956), pp. 120ff.

Chapter 6

1. Aldous Huxley, *Brave New World* (New York: Bantam Books, 1967), p. 30.
2. Ibid., p. 36.
3. George Orwell, *Nineteen Eighty-four* (New York: New American Library, 1964), p. 202.
4. Ibid., p. 225.
5. Ibid., p. 211.
6. Ibid., p. 220.
7. Robert Sheckley, "The Minimum Man," *Store of Infinity* (New York: Bantam Books, 1970), p. 82.
8. Ibid., p. 93.
9. Ray Bradbury, "Swing Low, Sweet Chariot," *Psychology Today* 2 (April 1969): 43.
10. Ibid., p. 44.

Chapter 7

1. George Seferis. "Argonauts" from *Mythical Story in Four Greek Poets: C. P. Cavafy, George Seferis, Odysseus Elytic, Nikos Gatsos.* Poems chosen and

translated from the Greek by Edmund Keeley and Phillip Sherrard, Penguin Books, Harmondsworth, Middlesex, England, 1966, p. 45.
2. Madame de Villeneuve. "Beauty and the Beast," in *The Arthur Rackham Fairy Book*. J. B. Lippincott Co., Philadelphia and New York (no date), pp. 49-65.
3. C. G. Jung. From "Psychology and Religion" in *Collected Works, Volume 11*, quoted in *C. G. Jung: Psychological Reflections*. Selections Edited by Jolande Jocoby, Harper Torchbooks, The Bollingen Library, Harper & Row, Publishers, New York, 1961, p. 214.
4. C. G. Jung. From "The Psychology of the Unconscious" in *Collected Works, Volume 7*, quoted in *Psychological Reflections* (1961) pp. 214ff.
5. C. G. Jung. From "Aion," in *Collected Works, Volume 9, Part II*, quoted in *Psyche & Symbol: A Selection from the Writings of C. G. Jung*. Edited by Violet S. de Laszlo, Doubleday Anchor Books, Doubleday & Company, Inc., Garden City, New York, 1958, p. 9.
6. C. G. Jung. From "Psychology and Religion," in *Collected Works, Volume 11*, quoted in *Psychological Reflections* (1961), p. 216.
7. Dietrich Bonhoeffer. *Letter and Papers from Prison*. Revised Edition, Edited by Eberhard Bethge, The Macmillan Company, New York, 1967, pp. 7ff.
8. Bonhoeffer, p. 8.
9. C. G. Jung. From "Psychological Types" in *Collected Works, Volume 6*, quoted in *Psychological Reflections* (1961), p. 208.
10. Mark Zborowski and Elizabeth Herzon. *Life Is With People: The Culture of the Shtetl*, Foreword by Margaret Mead, Schocken Books, New York, 1962, p. 149.
11. Martin Buber. *Tales of Hasidim: The Early Masters*, Edited The Curatorium of the C. G. Jung Institute, Zurich, Northwestern University Press, Evanston, Illinois, 1967, p. 157.
12. Nietzche. From *Thus Spoke Zarathustra*, quoted in *Evil*, Schocken Books, New York, 1961, p. 315.
13. Martin Buber pp. 109ff.

Chapter 8

1. Ernest Wood. *Seven Schools of Yoga: An Introduction*, A Quest Book, Published under a Grant from The Kern Foundation, The Theosophical Publishing House, Wheaton, Illinois, 1973, pp. 1–2. Date not given.
2. Patanjali. *How to Know God: The Yoga Aphorisms of Patanjali*, translated with a new commentary by Swami Prabhavananda and Christopher Isherwood, A Mentor Book, New American Library Inc., New Jersey, 1953, p. 126.
3. Daniel Noel (Ed.). *Seeing Castaneda: Reactions to the "Don Juan" Writings of Carlos Castaneda*, G. P. Putnam's Sons, New York, 1976, p. 59.
4. Baba Ram Dass. *The Only Dance There Is*, Anchor Books, Anchor Press/ Doubleday, Garden City, New York, 1974, p. 6.
5. Ernest Wood. For a discussion of the full range of schools of Yoga.
6. Baba Ram Dass. p. 118.

7. Lawrence Le Shan. *How to Meditate: A Guide to Self-Discovery*, Bantam Books, New York, 1974, p. 55.
8. Quoted in Le Shan, p. 59.
9. Quoted in Patanjali, p. 57.
10. Le Shan. p. 54. (my italics)
11. Baba Ram Dass. p. 120.

Chapter 9

1. William Butler Yeats. Quoted in *Yeats: The Man and the Masks*, by Richard Ellmann, A Dutton Paperback, E. P. Dutton & Co., Ind., New York, 1948, p. 280.
2. Fujiwara No Toshinari. Untitled Poem, in *One Hundred Poems from the Japanese*, Translated by Kenneth Rexroth, A New Directions Book, New York, 1964, p. 81.
3. Lao Tzu. *The Way of Life According to Lao Tzu: An American Version*, Translated by Witter Bynner, Capricorn Books, New York, 1962, p. 71.
4. Lao Tzu. p. 31.
5. Lao Tzu. p. 41f.
6. Heinrich Zimmer. *Philosophies of India*, edited by Joseph Campbell, Bollingen Series XXVI, Princeton University Press, Princeton, New Jersey, 1951, p. 120f.
7. Gerhard Adler. *Studies in Analytical Psychology*, Capricorn Books, New York, 1969, pp. 92–119. The "three-fold chronological pattern" is explored at length in his chapter, "Study of a Dream."
8. Michel de Montaigne. *Selected Essays*, Translated by Charles Cotton and W. Hazlitt, Edited by Blanchard Bates, Modern Library, New York, 1949, p. 563.
9. Sheldon B. Kopp, "My Own Dark Brother," *Voices*, Vol. 9. Number 2, pp. 60–61, Summer 1973.
10. Frank Haronian. "The Ethical Relevence of a Psychotherapeutic Technique, " *Journal of Religion and Health*, Volume 6, Number 2, April 1967, pp. 148–154.
11. Haronian. p. 152.
12. Erich Neumann. *Depth Psychology and a New Ethic*, English Translation by Eugene Rolfe, Harper Torch Books, Harper and Row, New York, Evanston, San Francisco, London, 1973, p. 21. (From the Preface to the Spanish edition, 1959).
13. Zimmer, p. 127.
14. Zimmer, p. 127.
15. Marcia Dienelt. "Fighting the Windmill," Unpublished, 1973.
16. Zimmer. p. 308, Quoted from the Sankhya Sutras, 4.1.
17. Zimmer. p. 310.
18. *The Song of God: Bhagavad-Gita*. Translated by Swami Prabhabananda and Christopher Isherwood, with an Introduction by Aldous Huxley, a Mentor Religious Classic, published by the New American Library, New York, 1956.

19. *The Song of God.* p. 125.
20. *The Song of God.* p. 44.
21. *The Song of God.* p. 46f.
22. *The Song of God.* p. 48.
23. Zimmer. pp. 160–162.
24. Arthur A. Cohen, *In the Days of Simon Stern,* Random House, New York, 1972, p. 346.
25. Cohen. p. 347.
26. Zimmer. p. 398, Quoted from the Swami Nikhilananda translation of *The Bhagavad-Gita,* New York, 1944.
27. *The Song of God.* p. 41.
28. *The Song of God.* p. 127.
29. *The Song of God.* p. 130.

Chapter 10

1. Quoted in *Alpha: The Myths of Creation* by Charles H. Long, Collier Books, New York, 1969, p. 38.
2. Sheldon B. Kopp. *If You Meet the Buddha on the Road, Kill Him: The Pilgrimage of Psychotherapy Patients,* Science and Behavior Books, Inc., Palo Alto, California, 1972, p. 76.
3. Mark Zborowski and Elizabeth Herzog. *Life is With People: The Culture of the Shtetl,* Foreword by Margaret Mead, Schocken Books, New York, 1962.
4. Erich Neumann. *The Great Mother: An Analysis of the Archetype,* Translated from the German by Ralph Manheim, Bollingen Series XLVII, Princeton University Press, Princeton, New Jersey, 1972.
5. Robert Graves. *ADAM'S RIB and other anomalous elements in the Hebrew Creation Myth,* with wood engravings by James Metcalf, Thomas Yoseloff, Inc., New York, 1958, p. 38.
6. Joseph Campbell. *The Hero with a Thousand Faces,* Meridian Books, The World Publishing Company, Cleveland and New York, 1949.
7. Erich Neumann. *Amor and Psyche: The Psychic Development of the Feminine, A Commentary on the Tale by Apuleius,* Translated from the German by Ralph Manheim, Bollingen Series LIV, Princeton University Press, Princeton, New Jersey, 1971.
8. Neumann. *Amor and Psyche,* pp. 4ff.
9. *Ibid.,* p. 26.
10. *Ibid.,* p. 85.
11. Arthur Waley. *Three Ways of Thought in Ancient China,* A Doubleday Anchor Book, Doubleday and Co., Inc., Garden City, New York, 1939, p. 16.
12. Elizabeth Gould Davis. *The First Sex,* Penguin Books Inc., Baltimore, Maryland, 1972.
13. Hellmut Wilhelm. *Change: Eight Lectures on the I Ching,* Translated from the German by Cary F. Baynes, Bollingen Series LXII, Princeton University Press, Princeton, New Jersey, 1973, p. 27.

14. *I Ching: The Chinese Book of Changes,* Arranged from the works of James Legge by Clae Waltham, An Ace Book, Ace Publishing Corporation, New York, 1969, p. 43.

15. *I Ching,* Legge & Waltham (1969), p. 44.

16. C. G. Jung. Quoted in *I Ching,* Legge & Waltham (1969) p. 14.

17. Alfred Douglas. *How to Consult the I Ching: The Oracle of Change,* G. P. Putnam's Sons, New York, 1971, pp. 25ff.

18. Kurt Vonnegut, Jr. *Breakfast of Champions: or Goodbye Blue Monday.* Delacorte Press/Seymour Lawrence, 1973, p. 209.

19. William McNaughton. *The Taoist Vision,* Ann Arbor Paperbacks, The University of Michigan Press, Ann Arbor, Michigan, 1971, p. 30.

20. Irene Claremont DeCastillejo. *Knowing Women: A Feminine Psychology,* published by G. P. Putnam's Sons for the C. G. Jung Foundation for Analytical Psychology, New York, 1973, p. 77.

21. Eleanor Bertine. *Jung's Contribution to Our Time: The Collected Papers of Eleanor Bertine,* edited by Elizabeth Rohrbach, published by G. P. Putnam's Sons for the C. G. Jung Foundation for Analytical Psychology, New York, 1967, p. 103.

22. Jill Johnston. *Lesbian Nation: The Feminist Solution,* Simon and Schuster, New York, 1973, quote from book jacket.

23. Donald Lathrop. Excerpt from unpublished personal correspondence, May 1973.

24. Oliver Schreiner. *Dreams,* Little, Brown and Co., 1922. Quoted in Bertine, p. 143.

Chapter 11

1. Dylan Thomas. "And Death Shall Have No Dominion," *The Collected Poems of Dylan Thomas,* New Directions, New York, 1946, p. 77.

2. Isaac Loeb Peretz. "Bontche Shweig," in *The Jewish Caravan: Great Stories of Twenty-five Centuries,* Selected and Edited by Leo W. Schwartz (Revised and Enlarged), Holt, Rinehart and Winston, New York, Chicago, San Francisco, 1965, pp. 342-348.

3. Heinrich Zimmer. *Philosophies of India,* Edited by Joseph Campbell, Bollingen Series XXVI, Princeton University Press, Princeton, New Jersey, 1951, p. 22f.

4. Edmond Rostand. *Cyrano de Bergerac,* Translated by Brian Hooker, Act V, p. 195.

Chapter 12

1. Rudolph Otto. *The Idea of the Holy: An Inquiry into the Nonrational Factor in the Idea of the Divine and Its Relation to the Rational,* Translated by John W. Harvey, Oxford University Press, London, 1950.

2. George Steiner. *The Death of Tragedy,* Alfred A. Knopf, New York, 1961.

3. Phyllis Hartnoll. *The Concise History of Theatre,* Harry N. Abrams, Inc., New York (Distributed by the New American Library, Inc., New York), An Abrams Art Paperback, no date.

4. Aristotle. *Poetics*, Translated by S. H. Butcher, Introduction by Francis Fergusson, Hill and Wang, New York, 1961, p. 52.

5. Northrop Frye. *Anatomy of Criticism: Four Essays*, Princeton University Press, Princeton, New Jersey, 1971, p. 214.

6. H. D. F. Kitto. *Greek Tragedy*, Methuen and Co., Ltd., London, 1966, p. 122.

7. Henry Alonzo Meyers. *Tragedy: A View of Life*, Cornell University Press, Ithaca, N. Y., 1956, p. 139.

8. Sigmund Freud. "The Psychotherapy of Hysteria," in *Studies in Hysteria*, Hogarth Press, London, Standard Edition, 1893, p. 305.

9. Aristotle. *Poetics*.

10. Friedrich Nietzsche. *The Birth of Tragedy*, Translated by Clifton P. Fadiman, in *The Philosophy Nietzsche*, The Modern Library, New York, no date, pp. 165–340.

11. Georg Hegel. *Philosoph of Right*, Oxford University Press, London, 1967.

12. Miguel de Unamuno. *The Tragic Sense of Life*, Dover Publications, London, 1954.

13. Sophocles, *Antigone*, Translated by E. F. Watling, in *The Theban Plays*, Penguin Books, 1971, pp. 126–162.

14. *Ibid.*, p. 127.

15. *Ibid.*, p. 128.

16. *Ibid.*, p. 133.

17. *Ibid.*, p. 133.

18. *Ibid.*, p. 136.

19. *Ibid.*, p. 138.

20. *Ibid.*, p. 139.

21. *Ibid.*, p. 144.

22. *Ibid.*, p. 145.

23. *Ibid.*, p. 146.

24. *Ibid.*, p. 146.

25. *Ibid.*, p. 149.

26. *Ibid.*, p. 152.

27. *Ibid.*, p. 153.

28. *Ibid.*, p. 155.

29. *Ibid.*, p. 150.

30. *Ibid.*, p. 162.

31. Rollo May, *Love and Will*, W. W. Norton & Co., Inc., New York, 1969, p. 123.

32. C. G. Jung. *The Archetypes and the Collective Unconscious*, from the *Collected Works of C. G. Jung, Volume 9*, Part 1, Bollingen Series XX, Princeton University Press, Princeton, New Jersey, Second Edition, 1968.

33. Sheldon B. Kopp. *The Hanged Man: Psychotherapy and the Forces of Darkness*, Science and Behavior Books, Inc., Palo Alto, California, 1974.

34. Rix Weaver. *The Old Wise Woman: A Story of Active Imagination*, Published by G. P. Putnam's Sons for C. G. Jung Foundation for Analytical Psychology, New York, 1973, p. 31.

Chapter 13

1. Gregory Bateson. "A Theory of Play and Fantasy" in *Steps to an Ecology of Mind*, Ballantine Books, New York, 1972, pp. 177-193.
2. Gregory Bateson, page 180.
3. Edward Albee. *Who's Afraid of Virginia Woolf?*, Pocket Books, New York, 1964.
4. Sheldon B. Kopp. *The Hanged Man: Psychotherapy and the Forces of Darkness*, Science and Behavior Books, Inc., Palo Alto, California, 1974, p. 48.
5. Carlos Castaneda develops this conception in detail throughout Don Juan series. *The Teachings of Don Juan: A Yaqui Way of Knowledge* (1969), *A Separate Reality: Further Conversations with Don Juan* (1971), *A Journey to Ixtlan* (1972), and *Tales of Power* (1974), Simon and Schuster, New York.
6. *The Hevajra Tantra*. Edited and translated by D. L. Snellgrove, Oxford University Press, 1969, Vol. I, p. 93. Quoted in *Mystical Experience* by Ben-Ami Scharfstein, Penguin Books, Inc., Baltimore, Maryland, 1974, pp. 23–24.
7. Jay Haley. *Strategies of Psychotherapy*, Grune & Stratton, Inc., New York, 1963.

Chapter 14

1. Martin Esslin. *Brecht: The Man and His Work*, New Revised Edition, Anchor Books, Doubleday & Company, Inc., Garden City, New York, 1971, p. xvi.
2. Robert Brustein. *The Theatre of Revolt* (An Atlantic Monthly Press Book), Little, Brown & Company, Boston, 1962, p. 263.
3. Bertolt Brecht. *The Threepenny Opera*, Grove Press, Inc., New York, 1960, p. 39.
4. O. Hobart Mowrer. *The New Group Therapy*, D. Van Nostrand Company, Inc., 1964.
5. St. Matthew 16, v. 19.
6. St. John 20, v. 23.
7. O. Hobart Mowrer. Pages 65ff.
8. St. Matthew, 6, v. 1–4.
9. O. Hobart Mowrer. Page 68.
10. Betinna L. Knapp. *Antonin Artaud: Man of Vision*, Discus Books, Published by Avon, New York, 1971, p. 11.
11. Peter Weiss. *The Persecution and Assassination of Jean-Paul Marat as Performed by the Inmates of the Asylum of Charenton under the Direction of the Marquis de Sade*, English version by Geoffrey Skelton, verse adaptation by Adrian Mitchell, Introduction by Peter Books, Atheneum, New York, 1965.
12. Peter Brook. *The Empty Space*, Discus Books, Published by Avon Books, New York, 1968, pp. 67–68.
13. Margaret Croyden. *Lunatics, Lovers & Poets: The Contemporary Experimental Theatre*, McGraw-Hill Book Co., New York, 1974, p. 240.
14. Peter Weiss. Act I, p. 31.

15. Simone de Beauvoir. "Must We Burn Sade?" in *The Marquis de Sade, The 120 Days of Sodom and Other Writings*, Grove Press, Inc., New York, 1960, p. 42.
16. Simone de Beauvoir. Page 3–64. (Originally published in the December 1951 and January 1952 issues of *Les Temps Modernes* and "Faut Il bruler Sade?"; translated into English by Annette Michelson.
17. Simone de Beauvoir. Page 64.
18. Sheldon Kopp. *The Hanged Man: Psychotherapy and the Forces of Darkness*. Science and Behavior Books, Inc., Palo Alto, California, 1974, p. 131.

Chapter 15

1. Walter Sorell. *Facets of Comedy*, Grosset & Dunlap, Inc., New York, 1973, p. 90.
2. Tom Wicker. *"One More Spring,"* an editorial. *The New York Times*, Friday, April 18, 1975, p. 31.
3. Michael Rossman. *"Music Lessons,"* *American Review 18, The Magazine of New Writing*, edited by Theodore Solotaroff, Bantam Books, Inc., New York, September, 1973, No. 18, p. 103.
4. *Ibid.*, p. 110.
5. *Ibid.*, pp. 106–107.
6. Janwillem van de Wetering. *The Empty Mirror: Experiences in a Japanese Monastery*, Houghton Mifflin Company, 1974, p. 128.